Alexa: 2018 Ama Guide

The Complete User Guide With Step-By-Step Instructions. Make The Most Of Alexa Today

<u>Now include The 250 Best Echo Easter Eggs</u>

Mark Smith

Alexa: 2018 Amazon Alexa User Guide

The Complete User Guide With Step-By-Step Instructions. Make The Most Of Alexa Today

ISBN: 1721202331

ISBN-13: 978-1721202331

Disclaimer

The information provided herein is stated to be truthful and consistent, in that any liability, in terms of inattention or otherwise, by any usage or abuse of any policies, processes, or directions contained within is the solitary and utter responsibility of the recipient reader. Under no circumstances will any legal responsibility or blame be held against the publisher for any reparation, damages, or monetary loss due to the information herein, either directly or indirectly.

The information herein is offered for informational purposes solely, and is universal as so. The presentation of the information is without contract or any type of guarantee assurance.

The trademarks that are used are without any consent, and the publication of the trademark is without permission or backing by the trademark owner. All trademarks and brands within this book are for clarifying purposes only and are the owned by the owners themselves, not affiliated with this document.

Alexa: 2018 Amazon Alexa User Guide

The Complete User Guide With Step-By-Step Instructions. Make The Most Of Alexa Today

Table of Contents

Introduction

There are so many different Echo devices today that a person could become overwhelmed trying to figure it all out. However, that does not have to be the case. If you are new to using Echo devices, if you have multiple devices, or if you just have a few questions than this book is for you.

This is the complete guide to using the Echo devices. Each topic that is covered is going to help ensure that you are able to use all of your Echo devices with ease. Written so that it is easy to understand and follow, this book will answer all of your questions about all of the Echo devices in your home.

From taking the Echo device out of the box, to walking through set up, all the way to learning how to create a smart home, and even a few Easter eggs, you are going to know everything that you need to know about your Echo device when you finish reading this book.

Why am I confident that you can use this book with any Echo device? Alexa is Alexa and Alexa is going to do what Alexa does no matter what device it is on. This means that the majority of the issues that you are going to face when you use Echo devices are going to be the same across the board. This also means that you can set up all of your devices using the same Alexa app, changing the settings, voice training Alexa and so on.

Because of this, you can rest assured that no matter what Echo device you have, this book is going to help you learn how to use it properly so that you can get the most out of it.

Chapter 1- Setting Up Your Alexa

Amazon Echo, Echo Dot, Echo Plus and Echo Tap Set Up

Knowing how to set up your Echo is vital if you want it to work properly, **the first thing that you will want to do is to download the Alexa App for your smartphone or other device**, however, you do not want to launch the app as soon as it is downloaded. Wait to launch it until you have unpacked your Echo and have plugged it in.

- Open up the Alexa app.

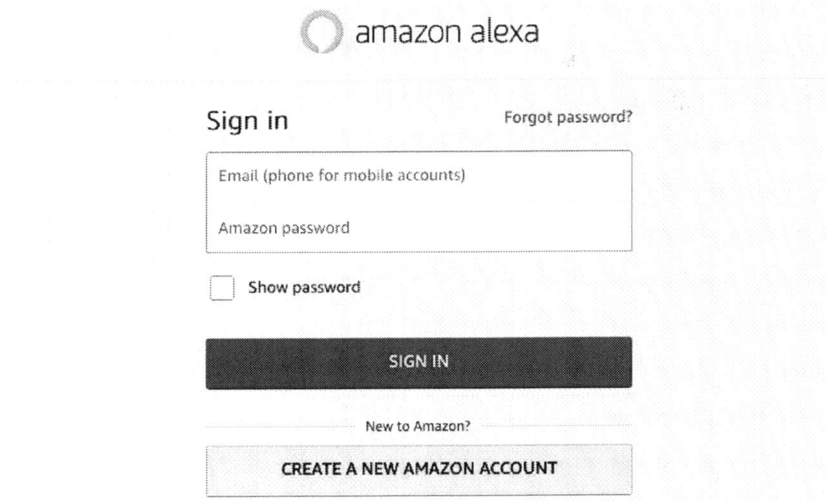

- **Choose a device to set up.**

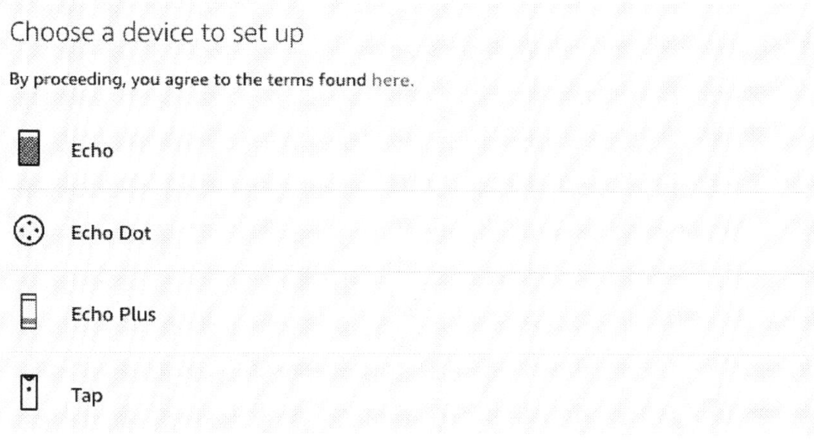

- **Choose your language.**

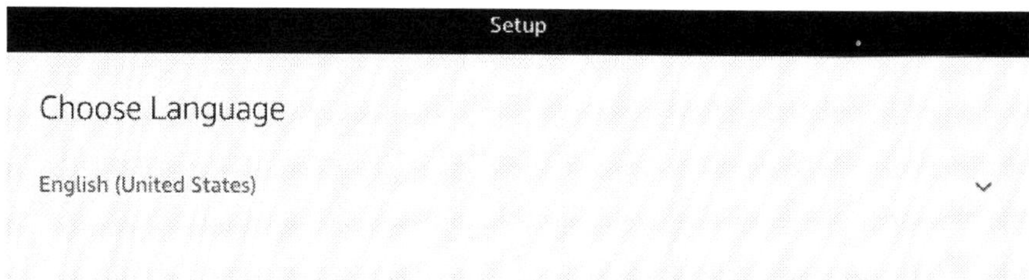

- Then the begin to set up Echo screen will pop up and just click on connect to Wi-Fi.

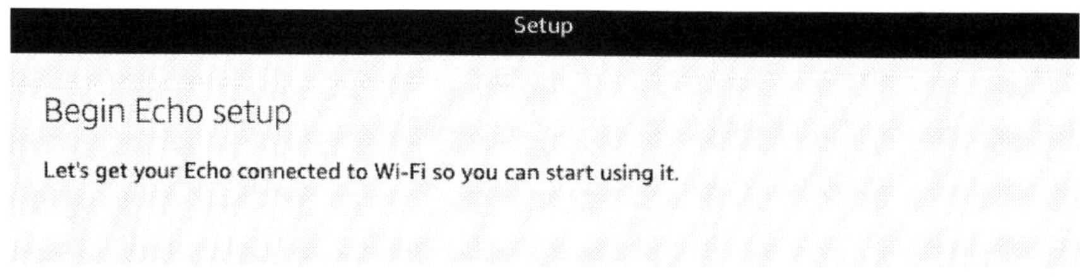

-

- Then wait for orange light ring screen pop up, you will need to click continue.

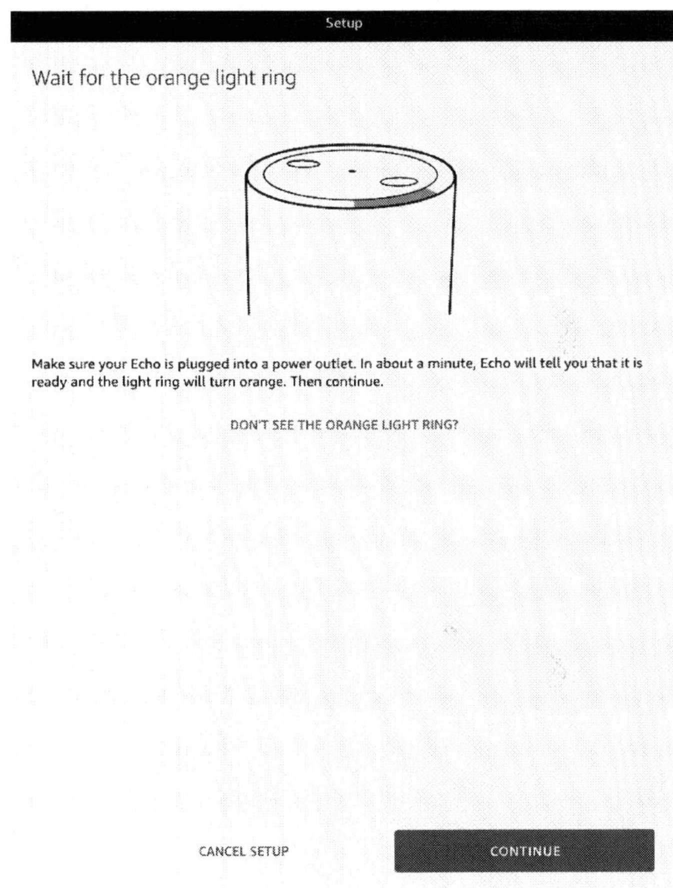

-

- The other screen will show up by saying connect your device, (iPad, iPhone and tablet) to Echo. At this time, you will need to go to your Wi-Fi setting and connect to the network that format as Amazon-xxxx.

- Now, you have to wait for your Echo says you are connected, and then return to the Alexa app.
- Once your return to the Alexa app, the connected to Echo screen is shown, and you just click on continue.

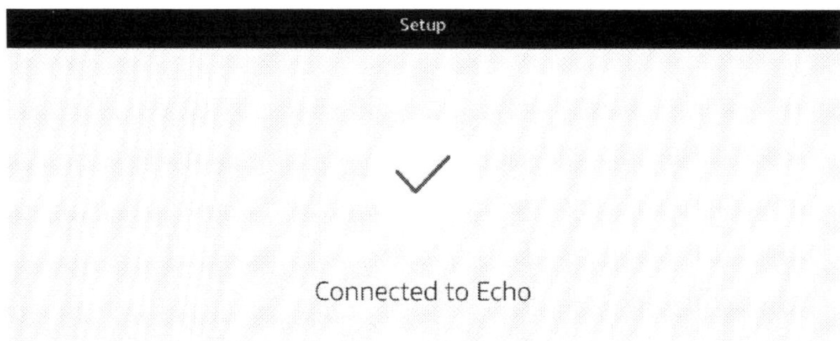

- You're almost done. The next step is to connect to your home Wi-Fi.
- After you connected to your home Wi-Fi, the set up complete screen will pop up.

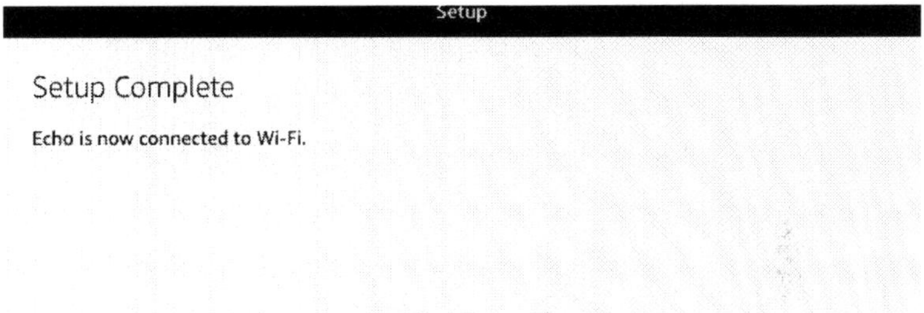

Setup

Setup Complete

Echo is now connected to Wi-Fi.

• Then you will need to click on continue, and the next screen will be the short video clip to show you about your Echo and how to voice command your Echo.

Intro to Echo

Now you try!

Say the following phrase aloud to Echo:

Alexa, what's the weather?

- Always say "Alexa" to wake Echo up.
- You can speak directly to Alexa. You don't need a remote.

Intro to Echo

All done!

Would you like Alexa to recognize your voice so she can personalize your experience? Create a Voice profile now

You are ready to start talking to Alexa. You can always visit Things to Try in the menu to repeat this guide or to learn more about things you can say.

Echo Show and Echo Spot Set Up

Setting up your Echo Show and Echo Spit is very simple and can be done in a few easy steps.

1. Just download and install the Alexa app on your cell phone or your tablet.

2. Now you need to connect the Echo Show or Echo Spot to the power supply, you will hear Alexa say," Hello, your Echo Device is ready for setup"
3. From here, you just follow the onscreen set up, you need to choose your prefer language, then connect to WIFI, next confirm your time zone and login in to your Amazon account, the last step is just read the term and condition and accept it. That's it. you are now ready to go.

It is important to remember that the wake word is Alexa however, if you want to change it to Computer, Echo, or Amazon you can do so in the settings of the app. You cannot however, pick your own wake word.

If you want to test your Echo, simply ask, "Alexa what is the time?" Alexa should then reply with the time.

How To Set Up Multiple Echo Devices

Knowing how to set up one Echo device is great but Amazon has created many different types of Echo devices in order to help you with all of the areas of your life. Amazon has actually made an Echo device for almost every room in your home. This means that if you love the Echo devices like most users do, you are going to need to know how to set up multiple devices.

But why would you need multiple devices? If you have multiple devices, you are going to be able to use Alexa in all of the rooms of your home. If you want to listen to music in multiple rooms on your Echo device, you do not have to move your device. You can also use your Echo devices as an intercom system in your home. The drop-in feature will allow you to drop-in on other rooms and speak to the people in them.

Finally, you can use your Echo devices to interact with friends and family members who have Echo devices as well.

Now before we get started it is important to understand that these directions are going to show you how to add additional Echo devices. If you have not set up your first device please refer to the previous directions as to how to set up an Echo device.

When you are ready to add an additional Echo device to your network you are going to be able to do so two different ways. The first way is through the mobile app and the second is by using the website alexa.amazon.com.

It does not matter which option you use because they are both going to allow you to add your Echo device to your network. Some choose to use the mobile app because they think that it is easier and provides them with more flexibility when it comes to changing the settings. There are also a few features that are only available on your mobile device.

1. In order to add an Echo device, you will either go to your app or alexa.amazon.com. You will then find the Hamburger icon which is located on the top left corner. This is the three horizontal lines. Click on it and then choose settings.

2. Choose the Set Up A New Device button which is blue. Choose the device that you want to set up. You will see the devices listed, Echo Dot, Echo, Plus, Tap, etc. Next you will choose what language you want to use. If you are not changing the language, simply click continue.

3. Next you will choose, “Connect to wifi”. It is important for you to make sure that your Echo device has been plugged in. In about 1 minute you will see the light on the device turn orange. When this happens, you will then choose continue.

4. Next you will go to the wifi settings on your phone or tablet and then choose the Amazon network. It will look something like this Amazon-1245. The network can take up to 60 seconds before it shows up so be patient. Once the devices say that it is connected, press continue.

5. All you have to do now is follow the directions that will appear on your screen. If you have a Wi-Fi password, you will be asked for it. Now you are ready for the next step.

6. Once you have connected your new Wi-Fi device you will want to set up the Echo device. In order to do this you will go back to the menu and then choose settings. You will find that there are four options here: Audio, Devices, General and Accounts.

7. Click on the devices section in order to set up the options for your Echo. From here you will be able to change the name of the device which is very useful when you have multiple devices. You can name them anything that you want however, if you have multiple devices, it is a good idea to name them by the room that they are in.

   In order to do this, you will choose the device that you want to edit. Scroll down your screen until you see Device Name and then choose edit. Type in the name that you want the device to be called and repeat the process for each of your devices.

8. Next, we will take a look at audio groups. This is going to let you set up Multi-Room Music. Begin by choosing audio groups and then going to settings. Choose Multi-Room Music. From here you will see three tabs. The tabs are called Devices, Scenes, and Groups.

   For right now we are going to focus on groups. When you use the other tabs, you will be able to focus on more advanced automation.

When you use the Groups tab, you will be able to choose combinations of your Echo devices so that you can control them all at the same time.

Tap on the Group tab. You will find 1 group already listed which is named Everywhere. Clicking on this is going to show that all of your Echo devices have been selected. You can deselect any of the devices however, while this is still going to be named everywhere it will not be everywhere any longer.

Instead of doing this, it would be better if you simply created a new group. Which we will talk about in just a moment.

There are benefits to using the everywhere option. It will allow you to play music throughout your entire house on each of your Echo devices, simply by saying, “Alexa, play (song) everywhere.” Alexa will then play the song on all of the devices.

If you have 3 or more Echo devices, you are going to want to create a few different groups. In order to create a group, you will choose the group tab. Next choose add group.

Find the amazon multi-room music group and then pick the name for your group. Choose next and then select which devices you want in the group. Choose save.

That is all that there is to creating a new group.

Of course, there are other features which you can use when you have multiple Echo devices such as the Drop-In Feature. However, we will talk more about these features later.

Setting Up Multiple Echo Users

Did you know that you can set up accounts for multiple users on your Echo devices? You can share your digital content and even collaborate on lists such as your grocery list.

The Amazon Echo devices can make your life easier allowing you to turn on the lights, order dinner, or turn on your favorite news station with just your voice. However, when you are sharing your home with many other people you will find that the to-do lists, calendars, and music choices vary greatly.

The great news is that you can set up multiple user accounts for your Echo devices. However, before you begin adding additional members, you are going to need to do a few things.

The first thing that you need to do is to ensure that the person you are trying to create a user account for has an Amazon account. If the person does not have an Amazon account, simply create one. You are going to need to use these account details in order to add the user profile to your Echo devices.

Adding a new profile will only take a few minutes. In order to add a new user to your Echo devices, you will use your Alexa app on your phone or tablet or you will go to alexa.amazon.com if you are using a computer.

Next you will go to settings and scroll to the bottom of the screen where you will find “Household Profile.” Click on household profile and then enter YOUR Amazon information.

Once you are signed in click continue and then have the other person enter their Amazon account information. Once the information has been entered you will then choose "Join Household."

When you have multiple user accounts on your Echo devices you are going to be able to share your content such as music and books, everyone will be able to add to the lists such as to-do or shopping lists and each person will be able to add to the calendars.

In order to switch profiles, you will simply say "Alexa, switch to (person's name) account."

I do have a warning for you before you add any users to your Echo devices. In order to add a user, you have to give them permission to make purchases on Amazon using your account.

In order to add a bit of security when it comes to purchases, you can go to the settings on the app and then choose voice purchasing. Choose "Require confirmation code," and then enter a code that is 4 digits which must be spoken aloud when a purchase is being made.

You may after adding a user to your household choose to remove them. Don't worry this is done very quickly. In order to remove a user, you will open your app or you will go to alexa.amazon.com.

Next, go to settings. Close to the bottom of the settings option, you will see a menu option called, "In an Amazon household with (and then the user name). You will choose this.

Next to your name you are going to see a button that says leave. Next to the rest of the user names you will see a button that says remove. Simply click on remove in order to remove the user.

How To Talk To Your Alexa For The First Time

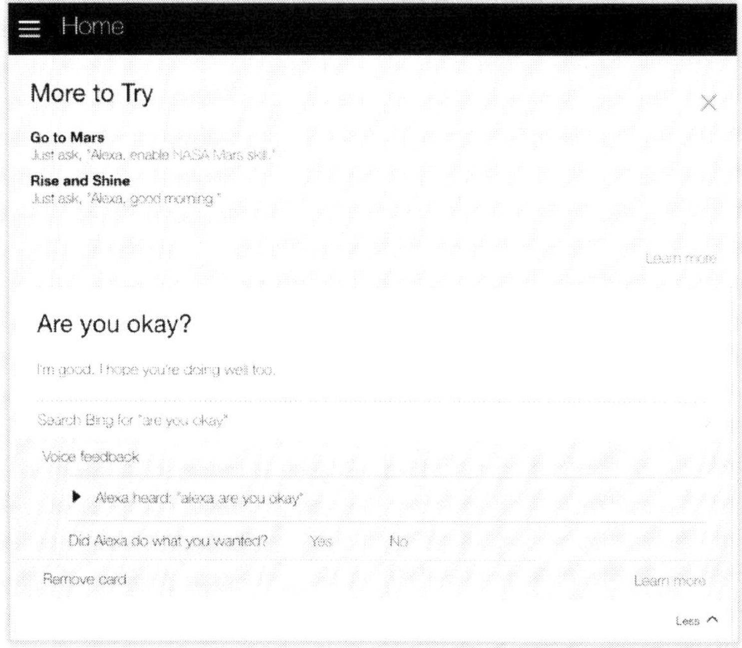

We will go through several other commands later on in this book, however, one command that you will want to know right away is "Alexa, stop." This is going to ensure that if you ask a question or give another command that will lead to Alexa talking a lot or too much noise, you can put a stop to it quickly.

Basic commands

- Alexa, help.
- Alexa, stop
- Alexa, let's chat.

- Alexa, mute or Alexa, unmute.

After you have spent some time getting to know Alexa, you may find that you want to change some of the settings. For example, if you want to ask Alexa about the news, you may find that you only want the local news or news from your favorite station.

In order to change these settings, you will open the app on your smartphone, scroll to the 'account' section and there is where you will be able to find the different settings that you can change. These include where your music will come from, what news you will get and you can even choose your favorite teams.

On top of this, you will be able to access your calendar, set your traffic updates and connect any other devices that you may have in your home. **Once you have done all of this, your Echo is completely set up and personalized.**

Chapter 2: How To Set Up Echo's Calling and Messaging

Amazon calling and messaging will work between any Echo devices no matter how far apart they are. The Echo will deliver your messages between devices, speaking them out on the speaker. It will deliver the messages to any Echo just as it would if they were on the same network.

The great thing about this is that it is that sending the messages is free. The calling feature includes conferencing as well as transcription and recording. The message recipients are going to get speech to text readouts via their Echo devices.

Some of the features take a bit of time to get used to. Therefore, I want to let you know how you can use Alexa messaging and calling with ease.

Set Up Step-By-Step

1. Download Alexa app on your mobile phone and open it.
2. On the introduction screen tap on " Get Started" to continue.

3. Then tap on your name.

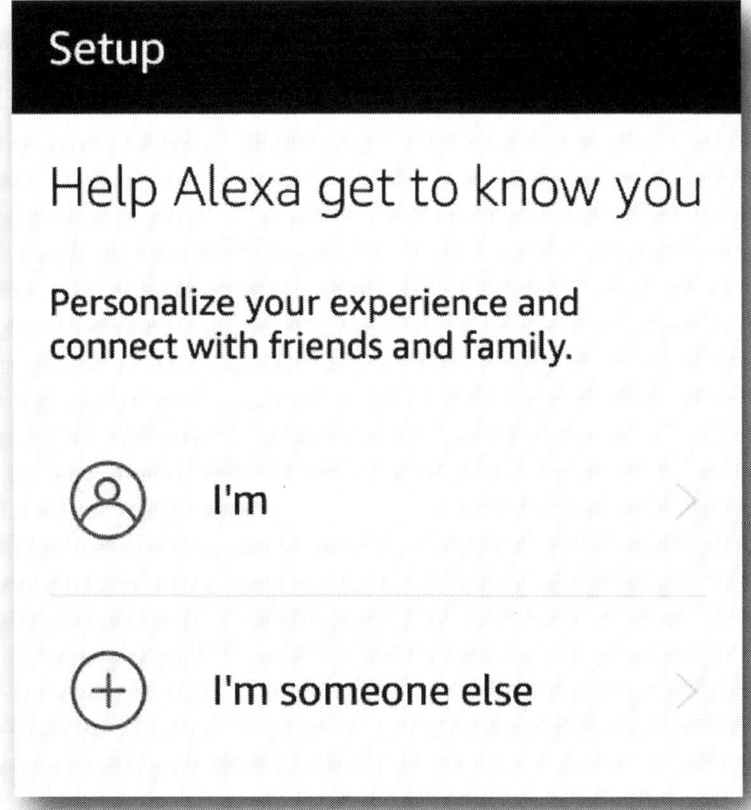

4. Confirm your name and click continue.

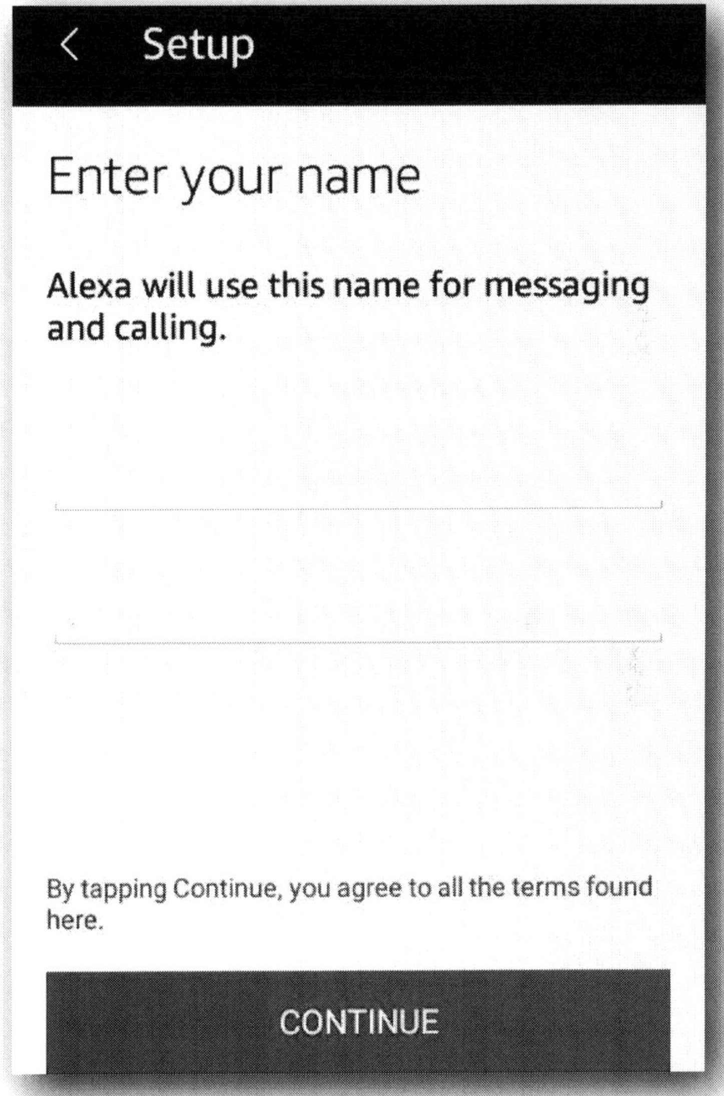

5. Give permission to Alexa app to access your contacts. tap " allow " to continue.

Setup

Give Amazon permissions

Contacts

Allow Alexa to periodically upload your contacts to the Amazon service, which helps you call, message, and connect with your friends and family.

LATER ALLOW

6. Now enter your phone number to associate with Echo. if someone in your phone contact set up this feature on their echo, their name will appear in the contact list on your Alexa app.

7. Then you need to enter the verification code and tap on continue.

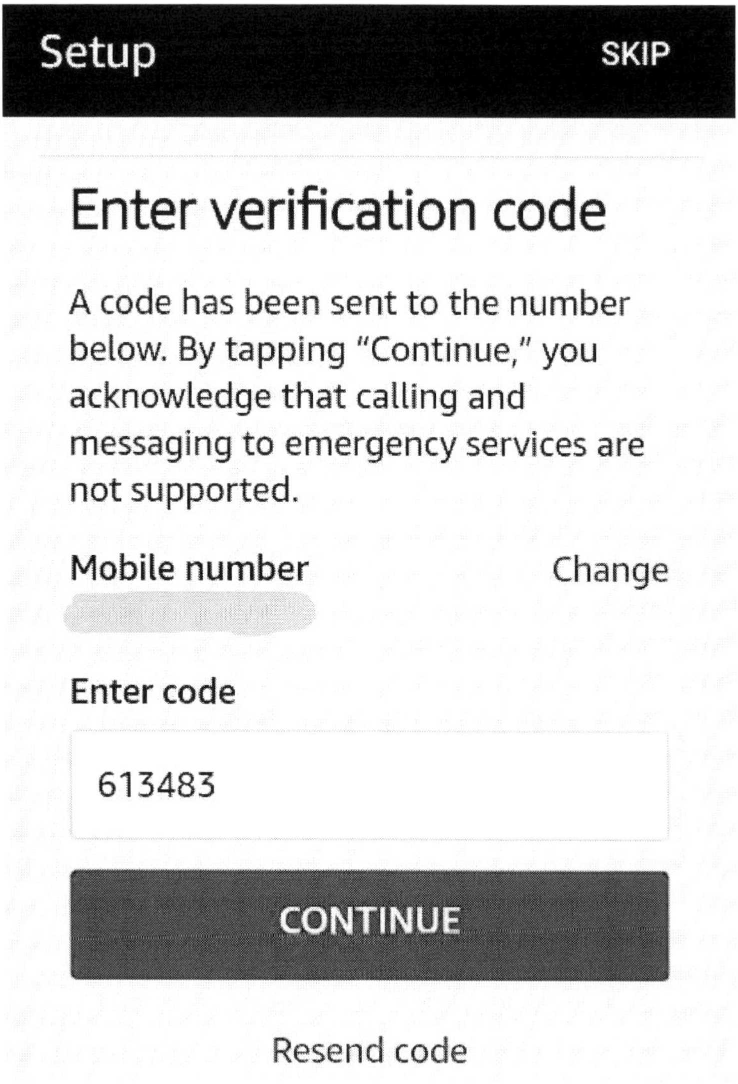

Setup SKIP

Enter verification code

A code has been sent to the number below. By tapping "Continue," you acknowledge that calling and messaging to emergency services are not supported.

Mobile number Change

Enter code

613483

CONTINUE

Resend code

8. When it's done. the conversations screen will pop up. this is where you can use your Echo's calling and messaging.

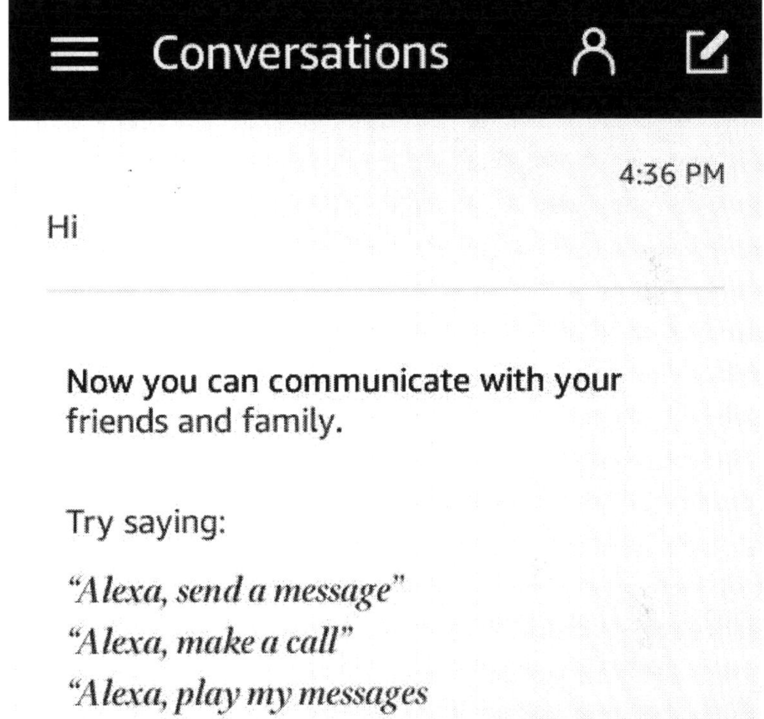

How To Call or Message Your Echo

If you are away from home, and if you want to call home. the Echo can be your home phone, just simply use your Alexa app on your phone and tap on your name, then you can call or message your echo. in addition, the other great function is you can leave a voice message to your Echo.

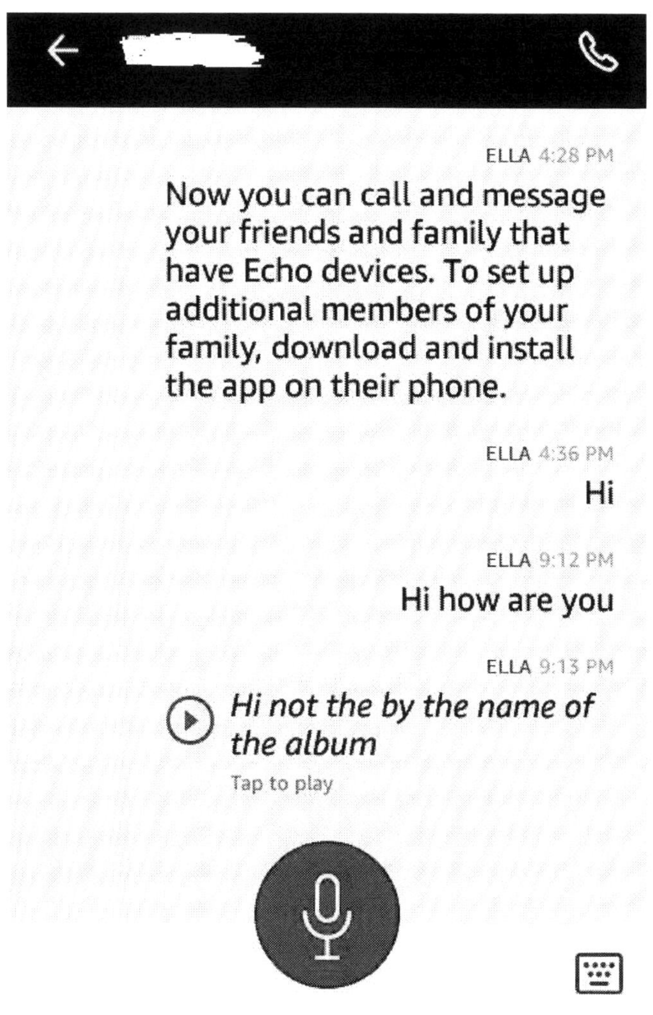

To answer the phone call on your Echo, just simply say," Alexa, answer the phone or Alexa, answer call."

To let Alexa read your message or voice message, just say," Alexa, read the message."

How to Call Someone

If you want to call someone in your contacts, just say the name on you contact. for example, " Alexa, call Steven."

If the person you want to call is not in your contacts list. you can say his or her phone number. " Alexa, call xxxxxxxxxxxx"

If you want to end the call. just say, "Alexa, hang up."

How To Message or Voice Message Someone with Alexa App or Echo

You can easily send message or voice message to other Alexa users using Alexa app or your Echo:

Alexa App: just select a contact and then tap on the message button, the conversation page will start, you can record the message or tap in your text message.

Echo: sending a voice message using your Echo is so simple, just say: “Alexa, message Richard. And the recipient’s Echo will light up and make a chime sound so people know that they received a message from someone.

Block Calls and Messages to Your Echo

Open you Alexa App and go to the contact list, you just need to select the person you want to block, and tap "block contact" button. That's it. you blocked this person and won't receive anything from them again unless you unblock them.

If you want to temporary block all message and call, use the "Do Not Disturb Feature" instead, just say "Alex, don't disturb me".

Chapter 3: All about Different Types of Echo You Can Choose From

Amazon has a whole new generation of Echo devices as well as services for its customers. The plan is to make the Echo an important part of people's lives and homes. In this chapter I want to go over some of the devices as well as talk a little bit about them. Each of the devices has its own benefits showing that Amazon has worked hard to ensure their customers keep coming back for the latest Echo device.

The New Echo

The first version of the Echo has been replaced with a new device that shares the same name. This new version of the Echo is just a bit shorter and just a bit wider than the original Echo. It also comes in three different finishes whereas the original Echo only came in one.

The new version of the Echo comes with a 2.5-inch woofer, Dolby and a tweeter which provides the user with a much better sound experience than the previous version. The multiple Echo speakers can also be connected in order to create surround sound.

Echo Plus

The Echo Plus looks much more like the original Echo however, the sound quality is much better. The device works best when used to control your smart home. The Echo Plus allows you to control all of your smart home devices without having to purchase a separate hub. When you purchase the Echo Plus, you will receive a free smart light bulb.

Echo Show

The Echo Show was unveiled in May of 2017 and it is the only Echo device that has a 7-inch touchscreen which allows for video calling as well as other visual content such as videos or music lyrics.

Echo Spot

This Echo device is a small round device which was designed to work mostly as an alarm clock. The 2.5-inch screen works like a mixture of the Show and Dot. Even though the screen is small, it can be used to stream videos and music as well as make video calls. You can also use the Spot to control other devices.

Echo Connect

The Echo Connect is basically a speaker phone that will plug into your landline port. The Connect will work with your home number. It will allow you to call other Echo as well as landlines and cell phones using your Echo devices.

Echo Button

This is an accessory for the Echo devices and not an Echo device within itself. It connects via Bluetooth to your devices and can be used to play many different games via the Echo device.

Echo Look

The Echo Look is known as the hands-free camera that works as a style consultant. It was made for the bedroom and allows you to see which outfits look the best on you. You can simply tell Alexa to take a photo and then the photos will be uploaded to the Look App. It is here that you can view the photos and decide what outfit looks best on you. You can also use the Look Book in order to see all of the outfits that you have worn.

Echo Dot

Now, the Echo Dot is only 1.6 inches tall, which is only the top section of the Echo device. It's half the price, **but it works in the same way,** and can do the same stuff as the Echo. This one was launched back in March of 2016, but it was made better when released in the UK.

The main difference is that the Dot doesn't have that giant speaker the Echo is. You have to hook it up to your own audio setup, and you can use it with existing speakers instead. The little speaker doesn't put out much audio, and is only really used for Alexa's voice.

The Echo Dot is good for those with a lot of Bluetooth connections, and can also be used for those that have larger homes and don't require everything to be in one space. If you have an office setup with many rooms, the Echo Dot is also a good investment, since typically they're available in packs of six or twelve.

What Echo Really Is

Amazon is making it easier with their Echo for their customers to order products from their website. Tell Alexa to order the newest movie that has come out, and it is done. Soon it will be in the mail shipping from Amazon right to your door.

Now, you don't have to grab a device, search up the product that you are looking for, compare prices and buy with one click. Now, Amazon will not have to be a destination, a place that you have to go to online to shop, but the storefront is going to be right in your house. With the convenience of ordering from Amazon, why would you take the time to order from anyone else? That is exactly what they are counting on.

Overall, the Echo can make your life easier. You can set up reminders which will keep you on track throughout your day. You can make a note of something when it pops into your mind without ever having to find a piece of paper or pen. You can have the information that you would normally read, read to you... imagine never having to read again! if you cannot afford a personal assistant, the Echo might just be right for you.

Chapter 4: How to integrate IFTTT with Echo

If This Than That… Means that if a specific event happens then a specific action will happen. Let's say for example you want to be alerted if there are certain events that happen in the news. You would choose specific keywords and if those words show up in news stories, those stories will be emailed to you.

Automating your life with IFTTT

Before you use the app, you are going to have to create an account at the IFTTT website. Channels include Dropbox, Google Drive, Instagram, Twitter, Fitbit and so on.

In the Do apps, you will create recipes, **these recipes are basically commands or formulas that the IFTTT will use to ensure the action that you want to be completed is completed properly.** The good news is that you can choose from recipes that have already been created or if you want, you can create your own.

Before we get into how to set it all up, let's talk about a few things that you can do.

- Email someone to let them know that you are on your way home. Want to let your family know that you are on your way home from a long day at work and ensure that they get dinner in the oven? By use IFTTT, you can ensure that you never forget to send that email.
- Turn your lights off when you go to bed at night without ever having to leave the bed. Love reading before bed, but hate getting up to turn the lights out?

You can choose a recipe for your Echo that will allow you to turn lights off, lamps and other electronics.

- Tweet on Twitter! Many of us are not very active on twitter or other social media, there are some of us that would like to change that. By using the Echo, you can create a repetitive tweet which will be posted every day. For example, 'Good morning,' or 'Enjoy your night.'
- If you already have a **To Do list** created in Evernote, you can use the Echo to add new tasks to your **To Do list**.
- Using the Do app, you can also add events to your calendar. You can choose to add something that will be repetitive, or you can choose to add a single task. The only problem that people have found with this is that because you are not looking at your calendar, you will not be able to see if there are events already scheduled for the specific time.

Setting Up IFTTT For The First Time

1. In order to set up the IFTTT, you will need to go to **IFTTT.com**. Of course, you should have an account already set up, however, if you do not, you will need to go through that process.

2. Once this is done, you will need to download the IFTTT app for your smartphone. You will then follow the directions that you will be given on the screen, setting up the channel. Once the channel has been set up, you will be ready to start creating your recipes.

3. **In order to start creating recipes, choose Amazon Alexa as your trigger channel. Next, you will choose the trigger, for this example, we will use** Tell Alexa to find your phone".

4. Now you will need to click on this recipe and turn it on by adding your phone number. Once it was set, you can now start to tell Alexa to find your phone by saying," Alexa, trigger find my phone". In addition, you also can create your own phrase, but remember you need to say" Alexa, trigger+ the phrase that you have defined.

Here are step-by-step instructions to get you started quickly and easily:

1. Download and open IFTTT App

2. Sign up with IFTTT

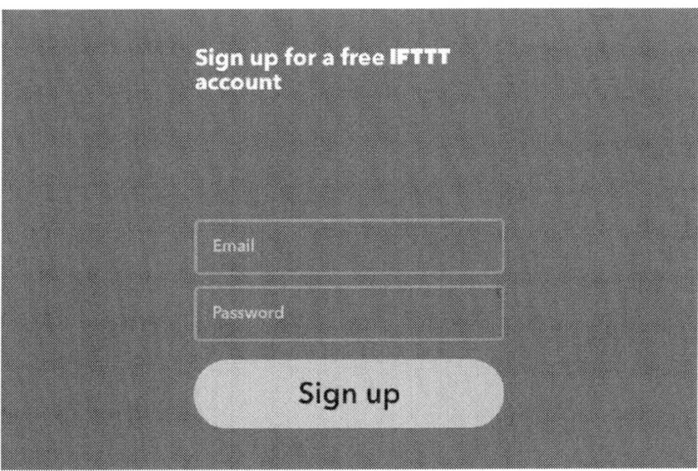

3. Search for amazon Alexa

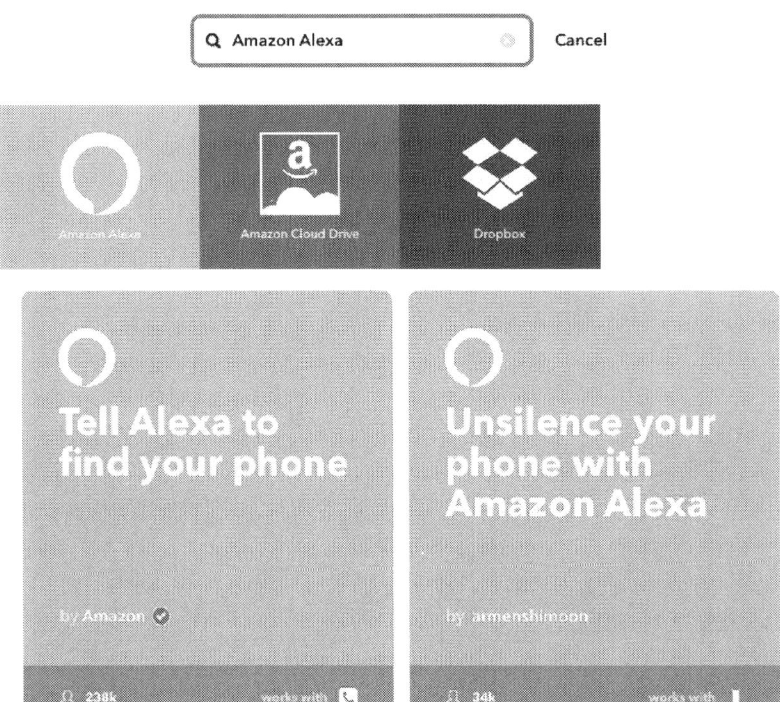

4 Tap on Amazon Alexa and then connect amazon account with IFTTT

Sign in to IFTTT using your Amazon account

Sign in

Forgot password?

Email (phone for mobile accounts)

Amazon password

Show password

Keep me signed in. Details

Sign in

New to Amazon?

Create a new Amazon account

Conditions of Use Privacy Notice

© 1996-2017, Amazon.com, Inc. or its affiliates

How To Set Up IFTTT to Find Your Phone

1. On the app looks for " Tell Alexa to find your phone" then tap on it.

2. Then turn it on and give permission to IFTTT to access your phone call.

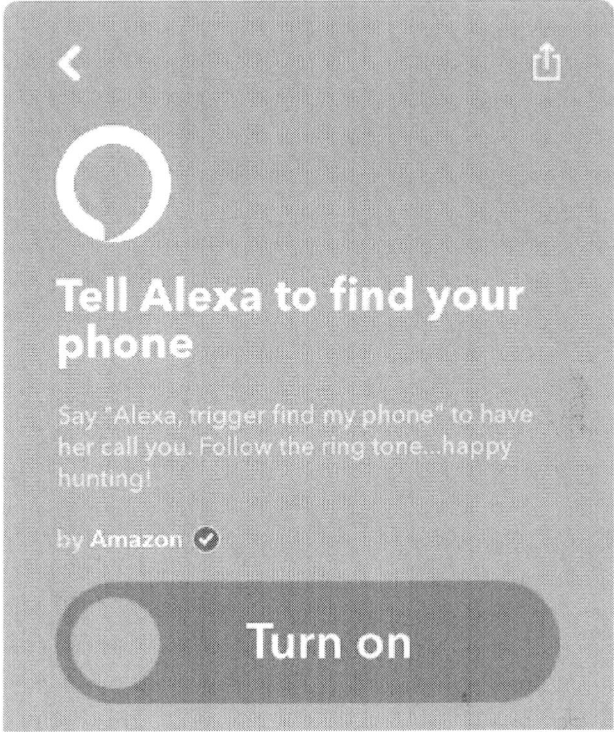

3. You need to provide your phone number and input the code which it sent to you to complete the set up.

Connect Phone Call (US only)

Enter your area code and phone number. We'll give you a phone call and share an activation PIN. Only US based numbers are supported.

Your phone number

Send PIN

IFTTT Smart Home Recipes

Asking Alexa to Lock Your Door

Tell Alexa to lock your door

Simply say, "Alexa, trigger lock door" to lock your SmartThings connected lock.

If you have SmartThings connected lock, simple use this recipe to lock your door by saying: “Alexa, trigger lock door”.

Tell Alexa to Put Your Lights On a Color Loop

Tell Alexa to start the party and put your lights on a color loop

If you have Philips Hue lights installed, just use this recipe to put your light on a color loop.

Set Your Nest Thermostat Temperature

Tell Alexa to set your temperature Via Nest. this recipe allows you to set the temperature of your home.

1. Turn on this recipe in IFTTT app.
2. Give the permission to Nest
3. Tell Alexa to trigger it by saying “Alexa, Trigger Nest to 72”

Start Your Robot Vacuum With Alexa

Tell Alexa to start your Neato vacuum

Use this recipe to start your Neato Vacuum, by telling "Alexa, trigger start my Neato"

Pause Your Kid's Internet

Just connect Circle with Alexa, and you will be able to tell Alexa to pause your kid's internet and have them take a break from their devices.

Ask Alexa to pause your kid's internet via Circle

The Best Echo IFTTT Recipes To Simplify Your Life

Email Your Shopping List

This recipe is very useful, you can tell Alexa to email your shopping list, so the next time before you head out the door, just ask Alexa to email the list, and it will be there when you arrive at the shop.

Tell Alexa to email you your shopping list

Sync To-Do List

This is an iOS IFTTT recipe, in your IFTTT app, simple just turn this recipe on and give necessary permission, now everything you add to your to do list on Alexa, it will sync with your iOS Reminders.

Sync your to-dos to iOS Reminders

ToDoist and Alexa

When you add a new item to your to-do list, it automatically updates the item to your todoist account.

Add your new Alexa to dos to Todoist

Keep a Spreadsheet of The Songs You Listen To on Echo

This recipe will add song name, artist name, album name and play time to your Google spreadsheet.

Keep a Google spreadsheet of the songs you listen to on Alexa

Receive a Notification on Your Phone When Your Alexa Timer Goes Off

Each time Alexa timer goes off, you will receive a notification on your phone.

Chapter 5: Voice Training Your Alexa & Set Up Routine

Just like any other voice assistant Alexa may have a hard time understanding what u say some of the time. If you feel like Alexa is not understanding what you say too often you may want to do a bit of voice training.

Voice training is only going to take a couple of minutes. Before you begin voice training you will want to take the time to consider a few things. It is important that you are completing the training under normal use conditions.

For example, if you have your Echo in your kitchen and you are normally giving commands from the other side of the kitchen, this is where you should do the training from.

It is also important for you to make sure that you are using the same voice that you use when you give a command. Do not try to speak more clearly than you normally do. Doing this is not going to help Alexa understand what you are saying when you give a command.

It is however, important for you to make sure that you have turned off any background noise such as the television to ensure that the Echo can actually hear your voice.

Now it is time to get started. Open up the Alexa app on your smart device and then choose the icon that is located on the top left-hand side of the screen. It is the three horizontal lines.

On the left side of the screen, click on setting and you will look for 'Your Voice. Follow the directions, you will read aloud less than 25 different phrases.

If you complete this training, you will be able to ensure that the Echo is able to understand what you are saying and you will reduce the number of times that it tells you that it was unable to understand the question.

How To Setup a Routine

The Alexa will let you create what is called a routine. A routine is going to have your Alexa complete several actions at a certain time or whenever you say a certain command.

In order to set up a routine, you will open your app on your smart device and then press the three horizontal lines to open the side menu. Next choose the routines.

Click create routine. Then create a trigger. Choose when this happens. Here you will need to decide whether you want something to happen when you say a specific phrase or at a specific time.

If you choose a specific time you will then set the time that you want the action to take place. Then you will choose what days you want the routine to happen. For example, one time a week, every day, weekdays, or only on weekends.

Make sure that the time is correct and tap done. You will then tap the plus sign in order to add an action. Choose the action which you would like Alexa to complete. For example, reading the weather, or turning on your lights. If you want a smart home action to take place you have to first make sure that the device is recognized by Alexa.

Now you will choose control device. A list of the smart home devices that you have will pop up and you will choose the device that you want to control. Then you will decide what you want the device to do.

Tap add to add the action to the routine. This is then going to bring you back to the routine page where you will be able to add more actions or choose create in order to complete the routine.

That is all that there is to it. Now you will be able to disable or enable the routine or edit the routine and name if desired.

Chapter 6: Shop on Amazon Using Alexa Voice Purchasing

Why Use Voice Purchasing

1. It's convenience if you are in the middle of doing something and just ask Echo to order the things that you need or run out.
2. You can also get Voice-exclusive deals that Amazon offers, which will save you some money.
3. On top of that, when we order with Alexa Voice, we are automatically eligible for free return shipping.

How To Set Up Voice Purchasing

You need 3 things to set it up

1. An Amazon Prime membership (Only for physical products)
2. A US/UK shipping address.
3. 1-Click payment method already set up in your Amazon account.

Voice shopping is already enabled by default in your Alexa app, you can enable and disable it by going to **Setting – Voice Purchasing.**

And the most important thing is setting up **a four-digit PIN (Go to Setting – Voice Purchasing)** to make sure that children don't accidentally order unwanted things without your permission.

How to Order Physical Products Using Your Echo

You have 3 options when you use Voice purchasing:

1. **New Products:** If you purchase something new, Alexa will suggest "Amazon Choice" products for you, if you like the products, you just need to tell Alexa to place the order.
2. **Reordering:** This is one of the feature I like the best, Alexa can draw on your order history and order the same items for you, and what you need to do is just confirm the order. It's done.
3. **Add to cart:** If you don't to order the items now or unsure about it, simple ask Alexa to add that products to your shopping cart and order them later.

Cancel and Track Order

You can cancel the order immediately after you ordered, and track the status of a recently shipped item.

Alexa Shopping Commands

“Alexa, track my order”

“Alexa, cancel my order”

“Alexa, reorder (the item name)”

“Alexa, order (the item name)”

“Alexa, add (item name) to my cart”

Buy Music Using Your Echo

Below are the commands to shop for and buy a song, album or shop for song by an artist:

1. “Alexa, shop for song (title)
2. “Alexa, shop for album (title)
3. “Alexa, shop for song by (artist name)
4. “Alexa, buy this (song/album)
5. “Alexa, Add this (song/album) to my library

Manage Your Shopping and To Do List

Adding Item To Your To do list

Here are the commands to add items to your to do list:

1. "Alexa, add [whatever words you want to say] to my To Do List"
2. "Alexa, what's on my To Do List?" Alexa will read the entries back to you.

Adding Item To Your Shopping List

Here are the commands to add items to your Shopping list:

1. "Alexa, add [Items] to my Shopping List"
2. "Alexa, add [Noun], It will understand and automatically add them to your shopping list.
3. "Alexa, what's on my Shopping List?" Alexa will read the entries back to you.

Edit and Delete Your Shopping and To Do List

1. Open your **Alexa app**
2. Go to **List**
3. Tap on "Shopping" Or "To Do" list, then select on the items you want to edit or delete.

Linking Your Any.do and Todoist Account

Any.do and Todoist is now integrate with Alexa app. To set them up, please follow the steps below:

1. Open your Alexa app.
2. Go to Setting
3. Tap on Lists, then pick Any.do or Todoist, Click on **Get Skill link**, and the last step is simple link your Any.do or Todoist accounts.

Now your Shopping and To Do Lists will be synced between your Alexa account and your Any.do or Todoist account.

Using the same commands:

1. "Alexa, add [whatever words you want to say] to my To Do List"

2. "Alexa, add [Items] to my Shopping List"

Chapter 7- Commands

Alexa can answer almost any question that you want to ask. “Alexa, how many days until Christmas?” The Echo will give you the answer… “Alexa, what can I use to replace eggs in a cake recipe?” The Echo will figure it out.

As you get to know Alexa more, you will find that you don’t need a lot of commands, you will be able to come up with them on your own, but when you are just starting out, you might need a few ideas and that is what I want to give you in this chapter.

Common Commands

- Alexa, stop.
- Alexa, volume three. * you can choose zero through ten
- Alexa, mute.
- Alexa, repeat.
- Alexa, louder.
- Alexa, unmute.
- Alexa, cancel.
- Alexa, volume down.
- Alexa, help.

Time and Clock

- Alexa, set the alarm for 5 am.
- Alexa, wake me up at 4 am.
- Alexa, set the timer for 20 minutes.
- Alexa, what time is it.
- Alexa, how much time is left on the timer?
- Alexa, what time is the alarm set for?
- Alexa, stop. (Used when the alarm is going off)
- Alexa, what is the date?
- Alexa, snooze. (Used when the alarm is going off)
- Alexa, cancel the alarm.

Music

- Alexa, what song is playing?
- Alexa, turn up the volume.
- Alexa, play softer.
- Alexa, volume ten.
- Alexa, stop the song.
- Alexa, pause.
- Alexa, next song.
- Alexa, resume.
- Alexa, buy this album.
- Alexa, buy this song.

Traffic

- Alexa, what is the traffic like?
- Alexa, how is my commute?

Weather

- Alexa, how is the weather?
- Alexa, what is tomorrow's forecast?
- Alexa, is it going to rain tomorrow?
- Alexa, what is the weather in Denver? (Or any city)
- Alexa, is it supposed to rain next Saturday?

News

- Alexa, what is in the news?

Shopping

- Alexa, add sugar to my grocery list.
- Alexa, add make a dentist appointment to my to do list.
- Alexa, send me my grocery list.

More Commands for you to try:

- Alexa, nice to meet you.
- Alexa, give me a tip.
- Alexa, what is the definition of {word}?
- Alexa, what is the population of {country}?
- Alexa, what is 10 kilometers in miles?
- Alexa, what is 5 dollars to Canadian dollars?
- Alexa, what is the square root of 25?
- Alexa, how many ounces are in a cup?
- Alexa, how far is it from here to New York?
- Alexa, who is the lead singer of Green Day?
- Alexa, why is the sky blue?
- Alexa, when is {title} playing?
- Alexa, tell me about the movie {title}
- Alexa, what movies are playing in {location} tomorrow?
- Alexa, what action movies are playing Sunday night?
- Alexa, what bakeries are nearby?

- Alexa, find the address for a nearby pharmacy.
- Alexa, find the hours for a nearby bank.
- Alexa, what's the weather in {location} this Sunday?
- Alexa, is it going to snow on Sunday?
- Alexa, will it rain tomorrow?
- Alexa, who won the {team or event} game?
- Alexa, how are the {team} doing?
- **Alexa, read my Kindle book.**

If you are looking for information on a specific topic, simply say, "Alexa, Wikipedia" and then the topic such as bento lunches.

Tips and Tricks

There are so many different ways that you can use Alexa, however, it can take some time to figure all of them out and that is why I feel it is important for you to have a few extra tips and tricks. I feel that everyone should know exactly how to use their electronics before they receive them in the mail, and not have to spend months trying to figure out how they work.

- Because the Echo does not accept an SD card of any type, many people fear that they will not be able to listen to their favorite songs however it is possible. By uploading up to 250 songs on the Amazon cloud player, you can use Alexa to listen to all of your favorite songs whenever you want.

- If you are a Prime subscriber, you can listen to all of the songs on your Prime Library.
- If you have ordered a package off of Amazon and you are wondering where it is, just ask Alexa. "Alexa, where is my order?" The package will be tracked and you will know exactly when to expect it.
- You can even order food. Simply tell Alexa to order your pizza from Dominos and the Echo will take your order, send it in and let you know what the status of your order is when you ask.
- Tell Alexa to discover your appliances and you can control everything in your home with the Echo. From your light bulbs to your television, Alexa can help you in every area of your life.
- **Don't have time to read your Kindle books? Tell Alexa to read your book to you while you work around the house.**

Reading Kindle Book: **when it comes to reading kindle, it's important that you do set up Alexa before you use it. To do so, do the following:**

- Go to " Music, Video and Books" and click on Kindle.
- Make sure you're logged into the kindle book

- Now, you can select your Kindle book on the screen to let Alexa reads for you.
- Or you can simply say what Alexa should read, such as "read Harry Potter" and it'll read a Harry Potter book for you.

Fun Things To Ask Alexa

If you find that you are bored and want to have a bit of fun with Alexa, try asking a few silly questions.

- Alexa, when is your birthday?
- Alexa, will you marry me?
- Alexa, do you know the muffin man?
- Alexa, tell me a story.
- Alexa, what do you want to be when you grow up?

Come up with any silly question that you want and see what Alexa has to say.

- If you want to access Alexa from the web, all you have to do is go to echo.amazon.com and you can control your Echo from there.
- If you want to mess with your family a little bit, simply speak commands into the remote while you are in another room and have Alexa say silly things to your family. Children love when Alexa talks to them and they are quite mystified by the Echo.
- If you need to figure out a math problem and don't have time to sit down and figure it out, just have Alexa figure it out.
- If you did not understand or hear an answer that Alexa provided for you, simply say, 'Alexa, repeat that."

- If all else fails and you need help from a human with Alexa, simply go to echo.amazon.com/#help/call. All you will have to do is type in your phone number and someone will call you to help.

Of course, this is not all that you can do with Alexa. In the next chapter, we are going to learn how you can use your Echo as a personal assistant to assist you in every area of your life.

Chapter 8- Using Alexa As A Personal Assistant

One of the things that many people love about the Echo is that it is a personal assistant that is always there, always working to make your life easier. By this point in the book, you may feel as if the Echo provides a ton of features that are a bit scattered, however, Alexa is not only a personal assistant, but a smart device and a little bit of the future in your home right now.

Alexa is always listening, however; no action is taken unless the command is given. Alexa can hear you even if you are a few rooms away, but it is even there for you if you are out of the house. You can control Alexa when you are away from home by using the app created specifically for your smart device.

As we have already learned in this book, Alexa can add tasks to your to-do list, update your social media status, and add events to your calendar, **but what else can it do for you?**

Because Alexa has access to your calendar, it can let you know when your first meeting of the day is, what projects are due on a specific date, what bills need to be paid, and even remind you when it is time for you to leave for work.

Calendar Setup

Did you know that it is possible for you to link different calendar accounts to Alexa as long as they are supported?

Once you have linked your calendar to Alexa, you can then have Alexa add new events or you can ask about the events that you already have scheduled.

You will first have to link one of the supported calendars. These include the iCloud calendar, Google calendar, Microsoft calendar, or Outlook calendar.

In order to link your calendar, you are going to have to first launch your Alexa app. Next you will go to the menu and choose settings. From here, you will choose calendar. A list will pop up from which you will choose your calendar.

After you tap on the calendar that you want to link, you will choose link. All you have to do from this point is to follow the directions that will pop up on your screen.

After you have linked your calendar, you will then be asked who can access the calendars. Finally, you will be able to ask Alexa about any events that are on your calendar or you can add new events.

Connect Echo to Your Calendar:

- Go to setting and click on Calendar.

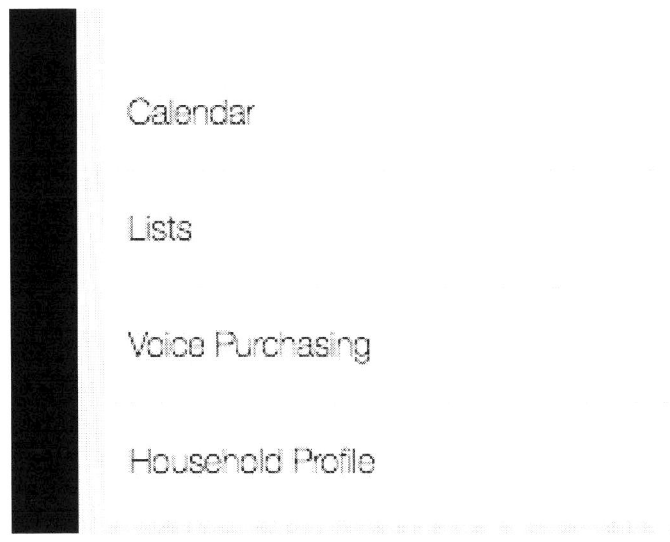

- Then link your Gmail account with Alexa by input your Gmail account information.

- After you finished linking your Gmail account with Alexa, now you can return to your Alexa app and place the check mark next to what you want Alexa to access in your Gmail account. Now it's done.
- To let Alexa tell you what is your next event or your calendar by simply **say " Alexa, what on my calendar? " or " Alexa, What's my next event? "**
- You also can let Alexa add an event to your Gmail calendar by saying" Alexa, add an event to my calendar" then she will ask you what day, time and name of the event.

Alexa is there to wake you up in the morning, to time your egg as it cooks and even tell you when it is time to head out the door. Alexa will let you know what you need to wear to work by telling you what the forecast is. You will never have to worry about being late to an appointment because Alexa can let you know exactly how long it will take for you to make it to an appointment.

Imagine what a difference it could make in your life if you could simply ask Alexa what you were supposed to be doing at any moment and it would be able to tell you. Imagine how much your productivity would increase and how much your stress levels would reduce.

Most of us create daily schedules for ourselves, but they end up just being lists that we have created, but with the Echo, you can have that schedule with you all of the time, ensuring that you are able to stay on track and help you get everything done that you need to get done.

Exactly how can we use Alexa to help us improve our productivity? Of course, we have already learned that you can use Alexa to add tasks to your to-do list, but you can also have the list emailed to you, printed out or read to you as you go about your daily tasks. This helps to ensure that when you get distracted, you will be able to get back on track because it gives you a sense of accountability.

You can also designate certain times for specific tasks and make your phone ring when your time is up. For example, if you know that you can complete a specific task or project in one hour, but you are finding that it is taking you longer because you are allowing yourself to become distracted, you can set the timer which will let you know when your time is up. When you set a specific amount of time for a task and you set a timer while doing that task, you are more likely to stay on task and you might find that you are actually getting done in a shorter amount of time than you thought you needed. What many people find is that just by doing this, they are able to double their production and Alexa can do it for you!

Because you are able to add information to your favorite computer programs, you can better track your money. Imagine how much easier it would be to tell Alexa to add a specific cost to your budget than to pull up your budget and do it by hand. This will make you more likely to track your spending and allow you to be more aware of where your money is going.

Have you ever gotten so busy that you just forgot to pay your bills? I think that most of us have been there and then we find ourselves having to pay late fees and maybe even taking a hit on our credit score. You can ensure that this does not happen by having Alexa set up reminders when your payments are due to ensure that you do pay them on time.

There really is nothing that Alexa cannot help you with when it comes to your day to day life. You can set up reminders for anything from doing the laundry to cooking dinner to completing work projects. You can ensure that you never forget an event at your child's school and that you are all around organized.

It is the lack of organization in life that causes most people to not be as successful as they want to be. It is because of this lack of organization that many people find it hard to get the things done that they need to get done each day. Imagine how different your life would be right now if you were completely organized and knew what you had to get done every minute of every day! Imagine just how much Alexa can help you!

Alexa In the Kitchen

While Alexa might be great at turning on the lights and ensuring that the doors are locked, it is even better at helping you out in the kitchen. Many people have chosen the Echo Show as their go to Echo device for the kitchen.

As soon as you take the Echo device out of the box and set it up in your kitchen you can start adding items to your shopping list or your to-do list.

For example, you can tell Alexa to add milk to your grocery list. You can also check your list by opening up you Alexa app on your smart device and choosing lists. Not only are you able to check your lists but you can have Alexa email them to you so that you can print them out and take them with you. No more wasting time making grocery lists or trying to figure out what you need to buy. When you run out, just tell Alexa to add it to your list.

Alexa can do much more than just add items to your lists. In fact, when you are cooking, you can have Alexa convert units of measurement for you. You do not have to download any skills in order for Alexa to do this. All Echo devices are able to convert units of measurement right out of the box.

You can even ask how much a cup of sugar weighs and Alexa will be able to provide you with an answer.

On top of this, you can use Alexa to set more than one timer. Have you ever been cooking several things at the same time and needed more than just one timer but found that you just don't have enough? Alexa can take care of the problem. You can set as many timers as you want and when you give them specific names you will be able to check and see how much time is left on each one of them.

Alexa can also start your coffee pot for you. Using the Smart Optimal Brew Coffee Maker, as well as your trigger phrase, Alexa will get your coffee going for you without you ever having to get out of bed. You do however, have to make sure that you put the coffee grounds and the water in the pot the night before.

Alexa is also able to control your smart small appliances as well as cooking devices. On top of this, you can use Alexa to control your large appliances such as refrigerators or ovens as well.

One very popular feature that many people use in the kitchen is Alexa's ability to provide you with recipe ideas. The Allrecipe skill is a very popular one because it allows you to ask for recipes that will work with the ingredients that you already have.

The Kitchen Assistant You Need

Now if you're into cooking, you probably would love to have someone who could help you with setting times, telling you what you need for a recipe, and the like. Well, Alexa is kind of the best non-human kitchen assistant you could need, and she helps you with food preparation a lot.

The big thing is she can take the measurements that you already have and convert them. not only that, she also tells you how to cook something without burning the food. Finally, if you're looking at a recipe online, and Alexa is supported, she'll be able to read off the recipe. This is a totally great thing that she does, and you'll be able to really get the job done fast.

1. **Just go to skills tab and do a search (recipe) and you will see a list of recipes skills.**

2. **Pick one, for this example, we choose (allrecipes) and click on enable this skill and link allrecipes account.**

3. **So now you can start asking Alexa for different recipes from allrecipes.**

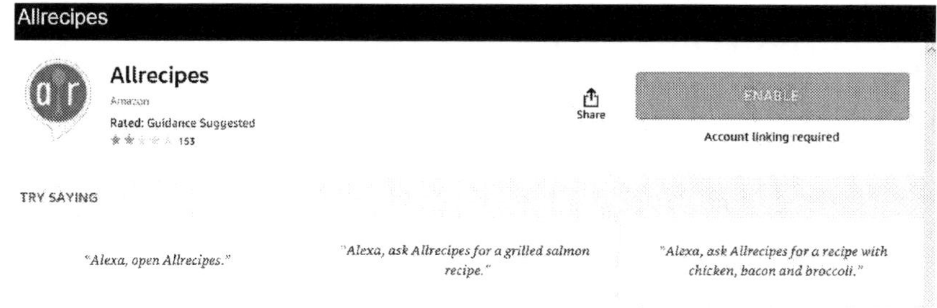
Allrecipes
Allrecipes
Amazon
Rated: Guidance Suggested
153
Share
ENABLE
Account linking required
TRY SAYING
"Alexa, open Allrecipes."
"Alexa, ask Allrecipes for a grilled salmon recipe."
"Alexa, ask Allrecipes for a recipe with chicken, bacon and broccoli."

For example, if you ask Alexa to set a timer for 20 minutes, she does so, and when it goes off, you'll be able to take the food out. If you're cooking dinner and want some help with it, Alexa help you choose the recipe. She can do this with so many recipe books it's not even funny, and in a sense, you just have to take care of the ingredients, and let her do the talking. If help in the kitchen is what you need, then Alexa can certainly do that, and so much more too.

In order to set Alexa as a kitchen assistant, you must do the following:

- Go to the skills tab

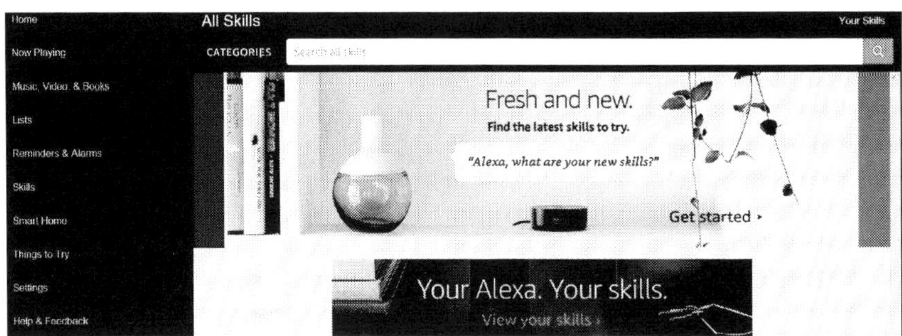

- Search "kitchen and recipes"

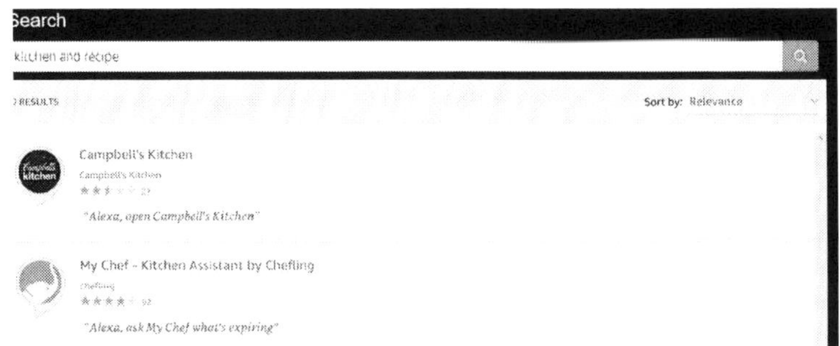

- Enable the skills to let Alexa access measurements, get recipes and other information.
- Also make sure that you have timers activated
- Tell Alexa how many minutes you need on the timer.
- Ask Alexa for the recipe that you need
- Tell Alexa what you need for that recipe and have her put it on the shopping list. By saying: Alexa add [something] to my shopping list.

It's as simple as that, and you'll be able to use Alexa to help with kitchen tasks.

Alexa and Fitness

Amazon is working very hard to make Alexa even more useful for its users and one of the ways that they are doing that is by ensuring that Alexa can help you in every area of your life and that includes your health and fitness.

Alexa is now able to tell you how many steps you have taken each day, how active you have been as well as how you have slept. All of this data is collected by a wearable device called the Fitbit. A simple command such as, "Alexa, ask Fitbit how I am doing today," will allow Alexa to access the Fitbit where it will be able to tell you how you slept last night, how many steps you have taken today, how many calories you have burned and Alexa will also be able to let you know if you need to walk more or if you need to get more exercise for the day.

The responses are also geared toward the time of the day that you ask. For example, if you ask how you are doing early in the morning, Alexa might tell you that you should try and take a walk, but not to forget to stop and smell the roses throughout the day.

Many people do not exercise because they do not know what they are supposed to do, but Alexa can help with that as well. Even if you do not have an hour a day to exercise, Alexa can help ensure that you are getting the exercise that you need to get each day. **Simply ask Alexa for a seven-minute workout and it will become your personal trainer, telling you what exercises you need to do in order to boost your energy, increase your metabolism and reduce your stress levels**.

Alexa is going to revolutionize the way that we exercise and how we look at our health. Not only is Alexa going to be able to help you track the amount of exercise that you do each day, but it will also help you to keep track of your calorie intake.

Alexa is now able to tell you how many steps you have taken each day, how active you have been as well as how you have slept.

Why are so many people overweight? Aside from the fact that they are obviously overeating and under exercising, most people do not realize how much they are eating or they underestimate a number of calories they are taking in each day.

I have already mentioned that Alexa can tell you the number of calories in the foods that you are eating but you can also have Alexa track the calories that you have eaten by using the food tracker. When you tell Alexa to track a certain food that you have eaten, it will give you a reply telling you that the food has been tracked as well as the number of calories that were in the food that you ate.

When you use this program with your Echo, you are going to become more aware of the food that you are eating as well as the nutrition that you are providing for your body. This is not just for those that are trying to lose weight, but for those that are habitual under eaters as well.

This program is going to be able to tell you not only how many calories you ate each day, but how many carbs, fats, proteins, and other nutrients that are vital to good health. The program is going to be able to show you if you are getting enough calories each day as well as if you are getting too many.

You are going to be able to track how you are sleeping as well. The way that we sleep at night has a huge impact on how we function the next day. When you use the Echo to track your health, you will be able to track how many hours you are actually sleeping at night, how many times you are waking up and you will be able to understand if there is an issue such as sleep apnea which is causing sleep problems.

On top of all of this, your heart rate is going to be monitored. Imagine having a tiny trainer with you all of the time that not only focuses on how much you are exercising but on what you are eating, how you are sleeping and on your heart health. It is the perfect health monitor.

Alexa can tell you the number of calories in the foods that you are eating but you can also have Alexa track the calories that you have eaten by using the food tracker

Alexa In The Bedroom

The Echo Spot is the newest way to bring Alexa into your bedroom. The Spot is the second of the Echo devices to come with a screen as well as a camera. It is very similar to the Echo Show however it is much smaller and very good looking.

When Amazon created the Spot, the intent was to provide customers with an Echo device that they would keep on their bedside table or on their desk. The good news is that it does not work any differently than any of the other Alexa devices because no matter what device you use or where the device is located in your home, Alexa is still Alexa.

The Spot is a very good looking device and is about the size of a softball. The front of the Spot has a 2.5 inch touchscreen on it. The screen makes for very easy set up of the Spot. It usually takes only about 5 minutes at most to get it up and running.

Once the spot is set up it will run just like any other Echo device. It is a great alarm clock as well. You can have Alexa wake you up to your favorite music and then before you ever get out of bed, have your news briefing and weather forecast told to you. You can listen to relaxing music when you go to sleep at night or even your favorite guided meditation.

Alexa Will Transform Your Child's Bedtime Routine

Your child's bedtime routine is vital no matter what their age. As a parent, it is your job to teach your child about proper behavior, self-discipline and ensuring that when they are adults, they are prepared for what they will face.

Alexa is now able to tell you how many steps you have taken each day, how active you have been as well as how you have slept.

So many children are growing up without the necessary skills that they need in order to be successful in their adult life and one of those skills is creating a routine. By creating a bedtime routine, you are not only teaching your child an important skill but you are ensuring that you are creating an environment for them which will help them get the proper amount of sleep.

Or course, no bedtime routine is foolproof, there are going to be nights when things just don't seem to work out, but having a routine reduces the number of times that this happens. Having a bedtime routine is going to help your child transition from activity time to rest time more easily.

When you create a bedtime routine, you need to make sure that it is made up of elements that you are positive you will be able to stick to. For example, you don't want to get over excited and create some routine that may be fun tonight, but become too much for you to handle in the future.

A bath, book and snuggle time are great elements of a bedtime routine. Many parents find that they feel a bit tired themselves and this may be a sign that they need to get more sleep themselves. Some parents even use the end of their child's bedtime routine as the beginning of their own.

It is important for you to understand that just because you have created a bedtime routine, it does not mean that the routine cannot be changed if it is not working for you. No matter what type of bedtime routine that you create, you need to make sure that there are minimal distractions. This means that you should limit the amount of electronics that are used, television is not part of a bedtime routine, neither are cell phones or tablets. You have to make sure that you and your child are able to focus on relaxing and spending time together.

Most people find that the hardest part of having a bedtime routine is maintaining it and this is where the Echo comes into play.

One thing that is vital when it comes to having a bedtime routine is actually having a bedtime. It is also important for the children to know how much time they have left before bed. Instead of you being the bad guy and giving them a countdown to bed, let Alexa be the bad guy and ask her how long until bedtime. On top of having a countdown until bedtime, you can have a timer set which will sound each night when it is time to start the bedtime routine.

We all know how important it is for us to read to our children, but most of us know that there are times when this is just not possible. This is where Alexa can be a huge help. Alexa can actually read your child a bedtime story. Now, in no way am I going to tell you to let Alexa read your child a story every night, nor am I going to tell you that you should allow Alexa to replace you lying in bed with your child while they enjoy the story, but on those nights when you just don't have the time or if you are sick, Alexa can be a lifesaver and it can ensure that your child does not miss out on their regular bedtime routine.

By creating a bedtime playlist, you can choose what type of music your child will listen to as they get ready for bed. You may choose a few lullabies, or even some classical music to help your child start to relax as they take their bath or change into their pajamas.

Some people choose to have more than one Echo in their home, each of them connected to the same account. This is because the Echo can be used to provide white noise which means that having one in different bedrooms is going to help your child sleep better throughout the night. Some people choose to have one in each bedroom as well as one in a common area of the home. On top of white noise, you can use the Echo to talk to your child while you are in the other room.

By using the command 'Simon says,' the Echo will allow you to communicate with your child when you are not in the same room. Simply speak into the remote and Alexa will repeat everything you say after you give the command. This means that instead of you yelling through the house for your children to go to sleep, all you have to do is speak into the remote and have Alexa tell them to stop playing or to go to sleep.

Of course, you can keep your child's bedtime routine as a simple routine that does not incorporate any type of technology because this type of routine has worked for thousands of years and it will continue to work long into the future. However, we have technology to help us make our lives more simple and we all know that there are times when the Echo would come in handy when it comes to our child's bedtime routines.

Once your child's bedtime routine is done, there is no reason for you to not have one of your own and there is no reason for you to not use Alexa to do so. Alexa can provide you with meditation music, it can read your Amazon eBooks to you while you are relaxing in bed, you can listen to your podcasts as you pick up the house after the kids have gone to bed and you can set timers to ensure that you keep on track and go to bed at a proper hour.

Many of us have gotten caught up in our favorite television show, a great book, or our evening chores and found ourselves up far later than we should have been. Just as you would set a countdown for your child's bedtime, you can do the same thing for yourself, having an alarm sound when you have 15 minutes until bed or when it is time for you to find yourself in bed.

Alert, Timers and Alarms Set Up

When Amazon rolled out the much-awaited features, reminders and named timers, people were thrilled. While it was possible for you to set timers before, it was not possible for you to name them. Now that you can name timers it is more convenient for you to set multiple timers.

Setting up multiple timers on your Echo device really is hassle-free now. It is also great that you can easily cancel any timers that you don't need any longer.

Setting up a timer is very easy. You can also name the timers in order to manage them more easily.

Begin by saying your wake word. Next simply tell Alexa what timer you want to set up. For example, "Alexa, set a alarm for 5 A.M." Or, "Alexa, set a breakfast timer for 6 A.M."

You can set a timer for anything that you want and name it anything that you want. In order to check the timer just ask Alexa how much time is left until (and then say the name of the timer) such as breakfast timer.

In order to cancel the timers, all you have to do is say your wake word and then cancel (the name of the timer.)

You can manage your alarms and timers by using your Echo or you can also do so on your Alexa app. However, it is important to know that the timers and alarms are tied to the device that you set them on and they are not shared between devices.

- To do this, you go to the menu, select "Reminder and alarms" and then you'll be taken to the alert area.

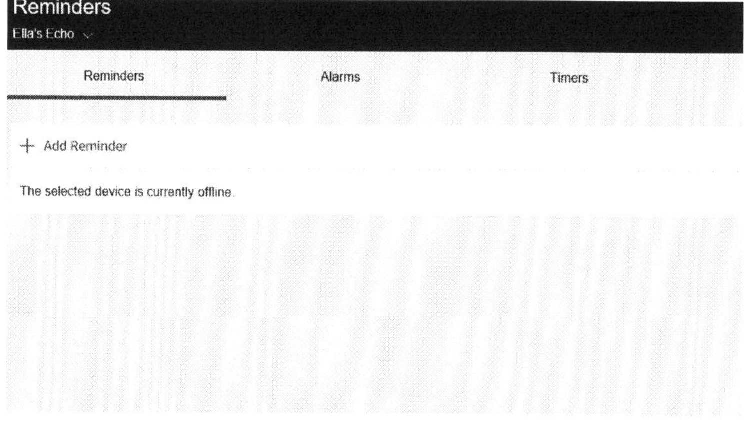

- There, you can set timers or alarms as you want. Or you can just use your voice to command your Echo by saying " Alexa, set timer for 5 minutes." or " Alexa, set alarms at 7 pm." You can then also tell the Echo to turn off after some minutes, or you can set timers for the future.
- If the alarm or timer ring and you want to stop it, just simply says" Alexa, stop"
- In addition, Echo has the reminder option. If you want to add the reminder, you just simply click on Add Reminder. It will ask you what do you want Echo to remind and what date and time.

Bedtime is not the only time that you can use the Echo to create routines. The most productive people in the world today understand how important it is to have a morning routine. They understand that they can get a huge amount of work done before 9 am. If you have the Echo, there is no reason for you to not use it to its full potential and have it help you not only create a morning routine but to help you stick to it as well.

With so many different ways for the Echo to help you throughout your day, there really is no reason that everyone should not have one. You don't have to be an important business owner to need a personal assistant, Alexa helps everyone from the CEO to the all-important stay at home moms, raising the next generation.

The Echo is for anyone that wants to make changes in their life, for those who feel that they do not have enough time in the day, for those who want to kick start a healthier lifestyle and everyone in between.

The Echo is for anyone that wants to make changes in their life, for those who feel that they do not have enough time in the day, for those who want to kick start a healthier lifestyle and everyone in between.

What Are Flash Briefings?

With so many new broadcasts to pick from, the flash briefing that Alexa provides has made it so much easier for us to listen to already recorded newscast. It is important to understand that the flash briefings are not live news but instead, pre-recorded.

You can listen to flash briefings from your favorite news stations as well as AccuWeather and several other stations.

In order to set up a flash briefing, you will go to the settings on your Alexa app and then click on flash briefing. From here you can choose weather updates, news, and even television shows. That is all that you have to do!

Traffic Details From Alexa

It is always a good thing to check the traffic report before you leave your house to ensure that you are giving yourself a new time or to make sure that you do not have to find a new route due to accidents or weather. Alexa can help you do just that. Alexa is going to be able to warn you if the roads are congested and Alexa can provide you with alternative routes as well.

Chapter 9: Echo Show, Tips and Tricks

It has been a few years now since the Echo entered our homes. Each of the devices has become almost a member of our family. Whenever we have a question, need help, or need to remember something our Echo devices are what we go to.

Many people are afraid of the fact that Alexa is always listening. The truth is however, that Alexa will begin listening when you say the wake word. However, it is actually possible for you to turn this off for a period of time if desired.

On your Echo device, there is a mute button. You can press the mute button and it will mute Alexa until you press the mute button again. You can do this when you are taking important phone calls or in the middle of a webcast to ensure that Alexa does not start spouting off when you are in the middle of an important task.

One of the most like features of the Show is the ability to watch videos. You can watch videos by telling Alexa to show you your video library or to search for movies with a specific actor in them. You can also tell Alexa to play a specific movie or a television show. When you want to pause the show or movie, all you have to do is say pause. When you are ready to start watching it again, simply say resume and it will begin to play again.

Speaking of movies, Alexa is able to tell you what movies are playing near you and Alexa can play the trailers for the movies so that you can decide just what you want to watch.

Enabling Do Not Disturb is a great feature if you do not want to be bothered. You can enable this feature by swiping down from the top of your screen. You will see DND off or on. It is here that you can decide if you are up for being bothered or not. If you tap the settings option you can create your own do not disturb schedule.

If you don't want to look at the default background wallpaper when you are not using your show, you can change the image by going to the settings option. You will scroll down until you see choose a photo, and select it. Next you will choose what image you want to use and you will set this as the wallpaper.

Many people love the Echo Show because not only are you able to hear your news briefings in the mornings but you are able to see them as well. If you ask the Echo Show for your news briefing, Alexa is going to show you the news with a video that includes audio.

One of the greatest things about the Echo Show is that it is going to help guide you whenever you need it to. For example, if you are making a special dinner but don't know how to make the recipe, don't worry, just ask Alexa and watch a step by step video on your Echo show.

When you use the Echo Show, not only are you going to be able to create tons of lists but you will be able to see them as well. If you want to scroll down but don't want to touch the screen, just tell Alexa to scroll down.

What happens if you lose your voice, or cannot talk for some reason but still want to use the Echo Show? If for any reason that you cannot talk, you can change the settings from voice commands to touch mode. All you will need to do is touch the screen in order to give Alexa the commands that you want it to follow.

Need to take a quick snapshot but don't have a phone nearby? All you have to do is tell Alexa to take the photo for you. If you want to take a sticker photo, all you have to do is to tell Alexa to do so!

No matter what screen you are on when you are using the Echo Show, all you have to do in order to get to the home screen is to tell Alexa to go home. Of course, you can use the touch screen, swiping down from the top and tapping the Home icon.

If you have not read the insert that came with your Echo Show than it is likely that you do not know where the on-screen menu is. In order to find the on-screen menu, all you have to do is to swipe down from the top of the touch screen and it will appear.

One of the things that many people do not like about the Echo Show is that it does not rotate. This can become annoying if you regularly want to change the direction that the Show is facing. If this is a problem that you find yourself dealing with, simply place the Show on an inexpensive turntable in order to remedy it.

Did you know that you can have Alexa display your album which will make the Show look like a digital picture frame? All you have to do is tell Alexa to show (whatever the name of the album is) and the pictures will show on the screen in slideshow form. If you want to adjust the speed of the slideshow, simply tap settings and then go to display.

We already talked about how you can use a photo as the home screen background but what many people do not know is that they can use an album as well. All you have to do is go to your settings menu then go to home screen. Tap background and then choose the album that you would like to use.

Many people have been talking about how bright the Show screen is and have stated that this is the reason that they will not put it in their bedrooms. However, it is possible for you to dim your screen. The screen is going to automatically dim when there is no activity, unless of course you are watching a video.

The screen will also automatically dim when have the do not disturb setting turned on. This means that if you want to have the Echo Show in your bedroom, you can turn on the **do not disturb setting** from 10:30 or whatever time to go to be until whatever time you get up and the screen will be dim. It will go back to its normal brightness when you talk to Alexa or touch the screen.

You can also force the screen to dim simply by telling Alexa to turn off the screen. There is also a dimmer switch which is located on the main menu that you can access by swiping down from the top of the screen.

Chapter 10- Alexa Skills

A Skill for the Echo is like an App for your smart device. The Echo, just like other smart devices comes with built in skills that include answering questions, accessing Wikipedia, playing music and providing the forecast.

Of course, there are tons of other skills that you can download and put to work for you in your day to day life. In this chapter, I want to talk to you about a few different skills that are popular with the Echo as well as how you can use them.

Now, with some of these skills, you'll need to have an account or subscription. **For example, say you want Alexa to request an uber for you. what you do is you log in with the uber account in the skills section before you use it. To do this, just follow the steps below:**

- Go to the skills tab
- Search for Uber in the search box at the top
- Then you will need to click on "Enable" to enable this skill and Link your Uber account.

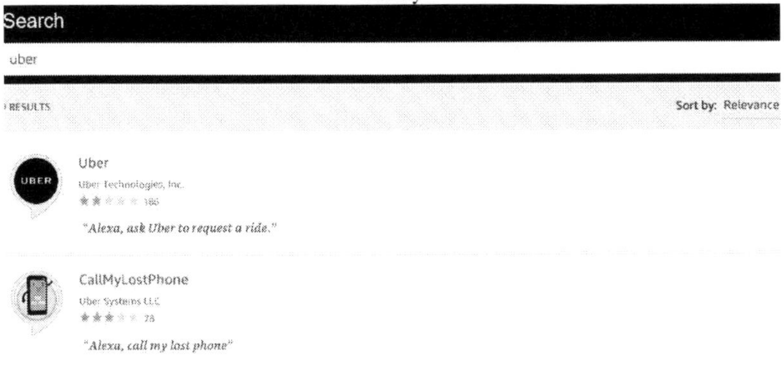

- You can then say "Alexa, request an Uber for me at 8 pm" and it'll do it for you.

Popular Health and Fitness Skills

Relaxing Sounds: Spa Music

Spa Music will help you feel relaxed. Try it when you feel stressed.

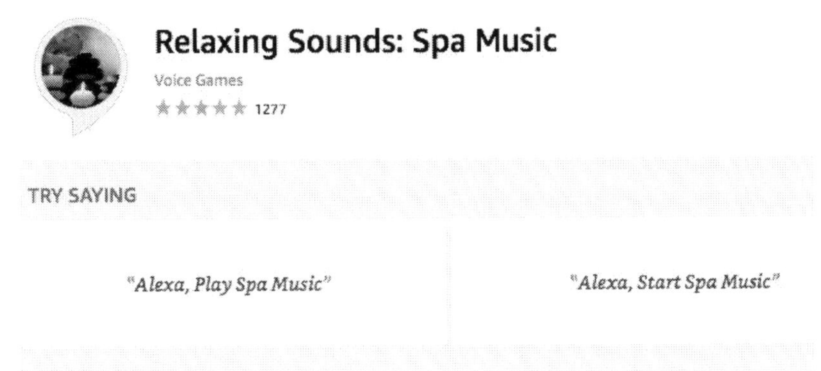

The Fitbit skill

is one that we have talked a little bit about in previous chapters. This skill can help you to track your fitness, the number of steps that you have taken, your sleep habits and even your health goals.

One problem that many people find with this skill is that it does not allow for more than one account which means that instead of the entire family being able to use the skill, only one person can.

This skill has great potential and as Amazon is making the Echo better, Fitbit is sure to improve the skill as well.

This skill is a great way for you to kick start a healthy lifestyle and help you get motivated to change the way that you are living right now.

To do this, simply do the following:

- Go to the skills tab and enable "Fitbit".
- Then you need to link your Fitbit account with Alexa.
- Put in your Fitbit information. Now you can start using it.

7-Minutes Workout

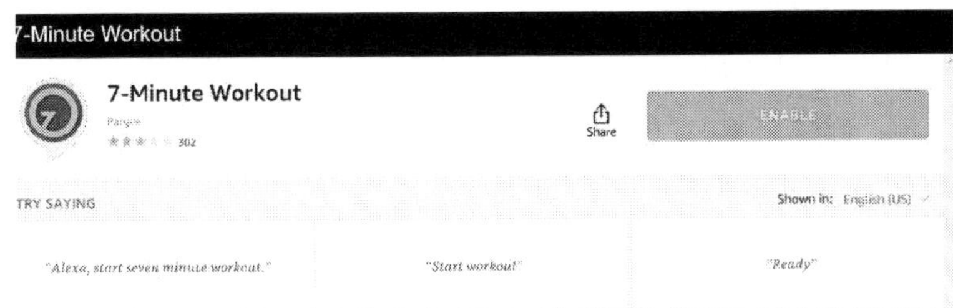

You are going to love this skill, it is a proven set of exercise that can improve your energy, lower your stress level and increase your metabolism. The workout just needs 7-minutes, you can tell Alexa, "Start 7-minutes workout" and it will guide you through the exercise, simple and easy.

Daily Affirmation

Need daily affirmation to help you start your day, get this "Daily Affirmation Skill", it can have a positive effect on your conscious and subconscious mind. Try it and you will love it.

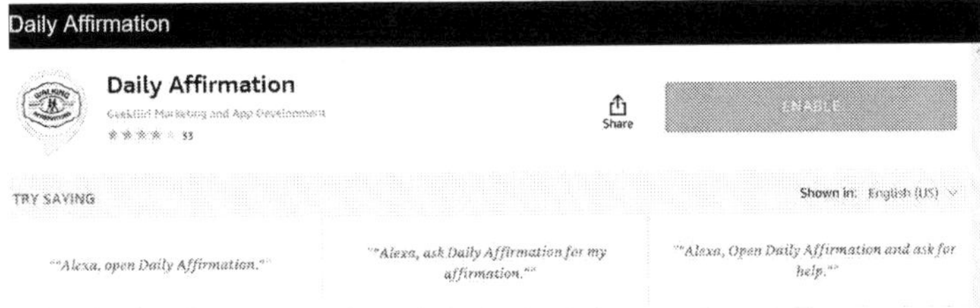

KidsMD

It is a skill that was created by Children's Hospital in Boston and it will provide you with information about colds, flues, and fevers. It also helps you to ensure you are giving your child the proper dose of medicine.

Ocean Surf Sound

Ocean Surf Sounds for Sleep and Relaxation

Six Voices

★★★★★ 21

TRY SAYING

"Alexa, open Ocean Sounds"

"Alexa, play Ocean Sounds"

If you like ocean sounds, this skill is for you, it helps you focus and relax while working on a task.

Night Night – Light & Sound

Night Night - Light & Sound

VoiceCities Pty Ltd

★★★★½ 20

TRY SAYING

"Alexa open Night Night"

This skill can turn on Alexa's light, say a goodnight message and then play a short music for you to relax and sleep.

Minute Meditation

This is a short, guided meditation that can help you reduce stress and relax.

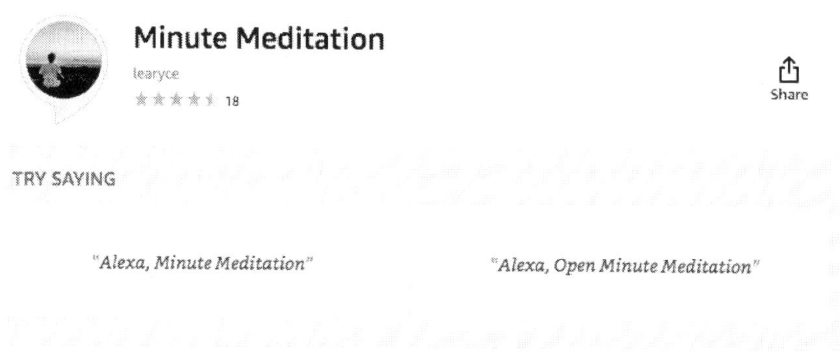

Nutrition Label

You can use this skill to ask for nutritional information on food.

Motivational Quote

This skill is very useful, it can give you a random motivational quote, use this when you feel down and need a boost to start you day.

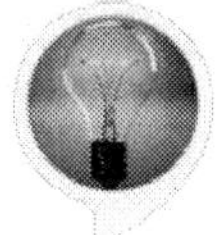

Motivational Quote Skill

Henry Garrett

★★★★½ 3

TRY SAYING

"Alexa Open Motivate Me"

"give me a quote"

1-Minutes Mindfulness

It is a skill that will allow you to choose from several background sounds such as rainforest or waterfall for one minute. The purpose of this skill is to ensure that you are taking one minute to be mindful.

Alexa Skills For Your Smart Home

SmartThings

It is one that most people will find more useful as it will allow your Echo to control your lights, the temperature in your home, your security system and other appliances.

TP-LINK Kasa

With this skill enable, you can interact with your TP-Link Kasa cam, lights and switches by voice.

Hue Skill

This skill allows you to interact with your Philips Hue lights, rooms, scenes, recipes and colors.

Nest Thermostat

Just enable this skill, it allows you to control your Nest thermostat.

Harmony

This skill works with your Logitech Harmony Hub. You can change channels, control volume and play/pause your content.

iRobot Home

If you have Roomba iRobot, use this skill to control it.

Popular Food and Drink Skills

Ordering Pizza

if you want Alexa to order something from Pizza Hut, you have to have your card information on there. To do this, just do the following:

- Go to the skills tab and search the restaurant. In this instance, we're using Pizza Hut
- Search for Pizza Hut in the search box.
- Once it shows, just click on it. then you will need to click on "Enable" to enable this skill.

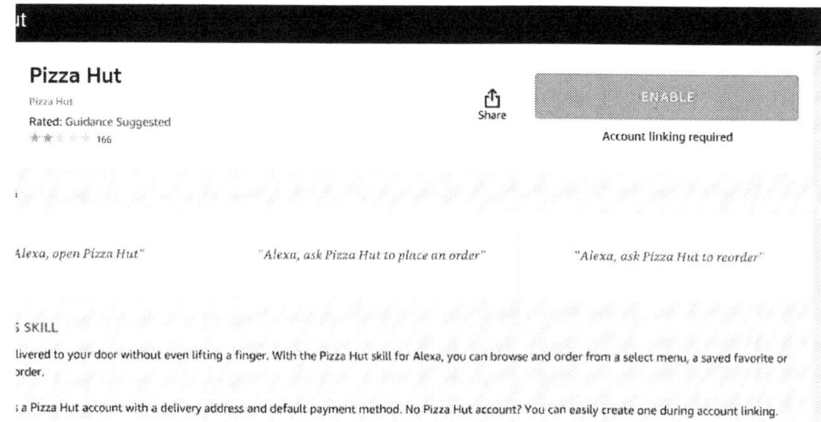

- After you enable this skill, you will need to link you Pizza Hut account with Alexa.
  - Log into your Pizza Hut ordering account and make sure that all of the card information is there and up to date.
  - You can now tell Alexa "order a cheese pizza from Pizza Hut" and she'll do that just for you

The Bartender

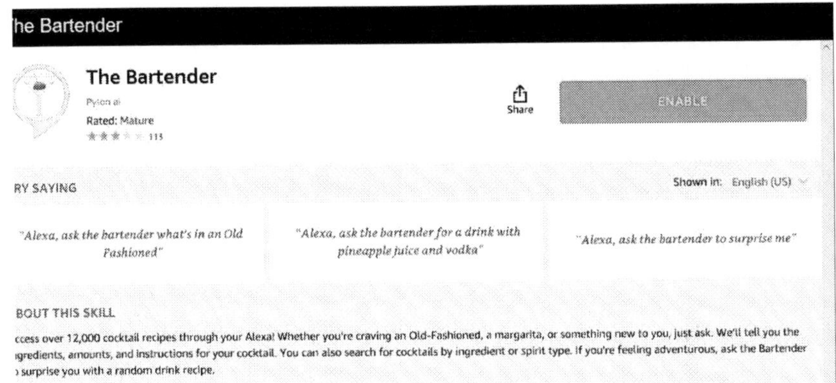

It is a very popular skill that will provide you with recipes which will allow you to make your favorite drinks right at home.

Some people do find that there are a few misinterpretations, but the skill can provide you with a large amount of recipes which is sure to please any crowd.

The Campbell's Kitchen

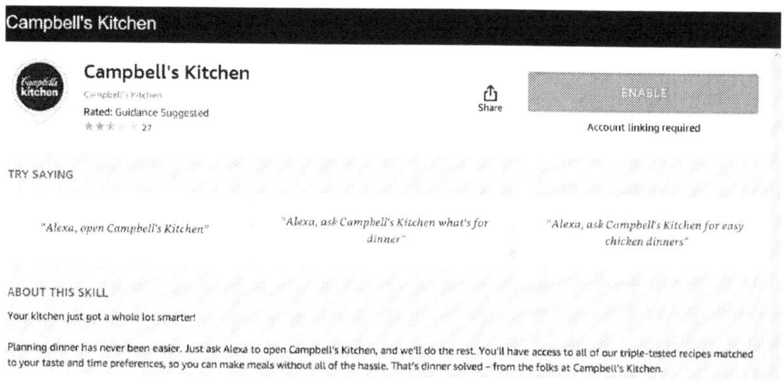

It is a skill that can help you out in the kitchen every single day. The app is trusted because it is from a well-known company and it can provide you with a ton of recipes. However, the recipes cannot be delivered to you via email which is one thing that many peopled do not like.

The Food Network Skill provides people with more recipes and even tips that come straight from the shows.

OurGroceries

If you have OurGroceries account, this skill allows you to add items to your shopping list. track recipes, scan barcodes and takes photos of the items.

OurGroceries

HeadCode

Rated: Guidance Suggested

221

TRY SAYING

"Alexa, ask OurGroceries to add milk to shopping list."

"Alexa, tell OurGroceries to remove olive oil from Walmart."

Allrecipes

It has 60,000 recipes. So if you don't know what to cook for dinner tonight, use the skill to find recipe ideas.

Allrecipes

Amazon

Rated: Guidance Suggested

169

Share

TRY SAYING

"Alexa, open Allrecipes."

"Alexa, ask Allrecipes for a grilled salmon recipe."

Top Alexa Skills

Jeopardy

If you are looking to build your knowledge, the Echo can help with that as well with skills such as **Jeopardy**, which is one of the most successful game skills. The quiz is not overbearing, but relaxing and allows you to answer up to six questions per day.

The Magic Door

This is a great skill for children and adults alike. This skill will allow you to create your own stories beginning with three settings, you are able to choose the direction of the story and the skill will provide sound effects as you create your story. Some people do feel that the stories are not long enough and wish that there were more options available, but it is a great way to get the kids to be a bit creative.

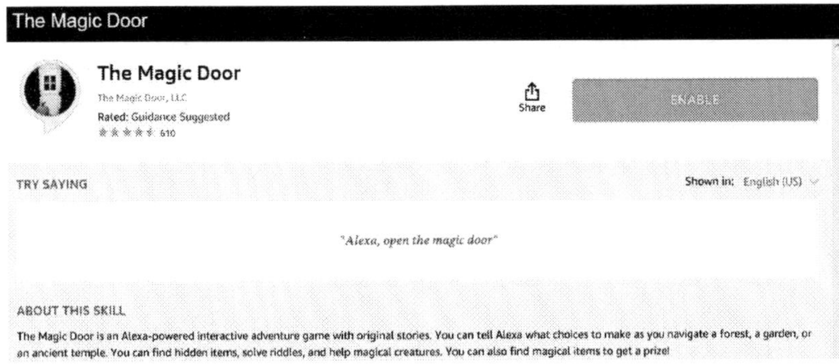

Question Of The Day

Use this skill to improve your cultural literacy, you will get new questions every day that you can respond to, for examples: arts, entertainment, literature and science.

Question of the Day

VoicePress.AI

Rated: Guidance Suggested

★★★★★ 1011

TRY SAYING

"Alexa, ask Question of the Day."

"Alexa, play Que

Yo Mama Jokes

It is a skill that does what it is supposed to do and it does it quite well, providing a large number of jokes that appeal to many different people.

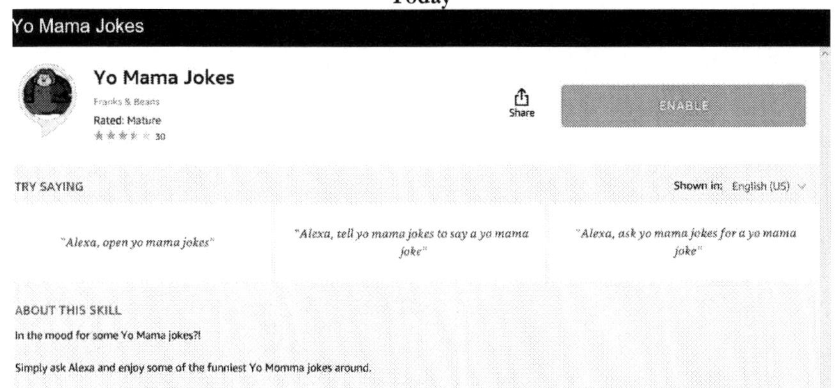
Yo Mama Jokes
Yo Mama Jokes
Rated: Mature
30
Share
ENABLE
TRY SAYING
Shown in: English (US)
"Alexa, open yo mama jokes"
"Alexa, tell yo mama jokes to say a yo mama joke"
"Alexa, ask yo mama jokes for a yo mama joke"
ABOUT THIS SKILL
In the mood for some Yo Mama jokes?!
Simply ask Alexa and enjoy some of the funniest Yo Momma jokes around.

The Amazing Word Master Game

This is a skill that is available and it is a word game with Alexa, however, some people have found that because of the limited vocabulary, it can get a bit repetitive and there are times when it does not recognize what you are saying. With all of the issues that it does have, many are saying that it is still one of their favorite games available through the Echo.

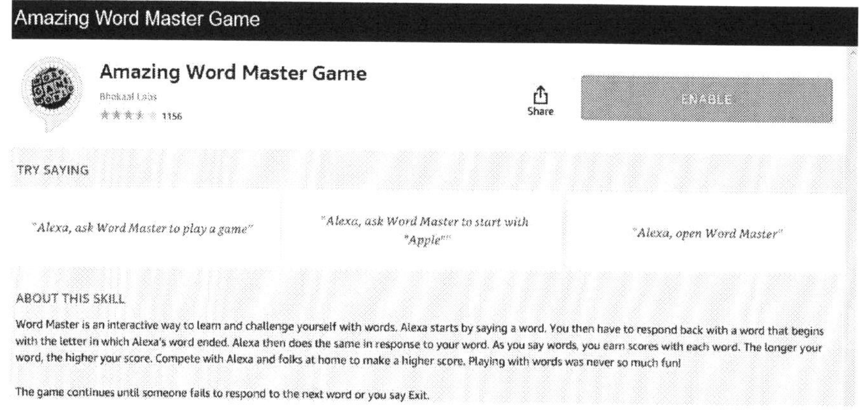

Of course, there are many other skills, including Audiobooks from Audible, timers, and alarms, sports updates, find your phone, and Bing just to name a few.

The fact is that there is a skill out there for almost everything. Amazon is working hard every day to ensure that the Echo provides the best experience for every owner and that it makes your life easier in every way.

Chapter 11- Amazon Alexa, Troubleshooting

In this chapter, I want to talk a little bit about troubleshooting your Amazon Echo. If you do by chance have a problem with your Echo, it is important that you are able to solve it quickly.

Alexa Can't Find Your Device

- This is the first of the major common problems with the system. You might want Alexa to do something with a system, but it doesn't. Your first thing to do, is to check to see if the device that you have is supported by Alexa. While the list of devices is growing, some of them don't support it, and that might be the problem.

- If you have a device that is supported, but it's not showing, you might have to add it. What you should do is open up the app for Alexa, go to the smart home area, go to discover devices, then your devices, and you'll see if it's there. If you can hook it up, do just that. if not, you can also go to a channel that has a list of supported devices. You might be able to connect it there.

- Now, if you have it added, but Alexa isn't recognizing it, there are a few solutions to this. The first is to look at your invocation. You might be saying the device a bit strangely, and Alexa doesn't recognize it. if that's the case, take a look at how it's being said, for you might need to be more specific with your commands.

- The other reason is that some of these systems don't stay connected for very long due to problems with the software, networks being crowded, and other issues. Some software goes offline for a few days, but it can be fixed by a simple power cycle (such as turning something on manually) to fix the connectivity. If that doesn't work, rebooting and removing and re-adding a device could also fix this.

Disconnects from a Network a Lot

- If this device doesn't really stay connected for too long, you can fix the connection as follows:

- The first, is to power cycle everything related to this, such as the router, your modem, and Alexa itself. Once you're done with that, try to stream something for a couple of minutes, and see if the problem is still there. If so, it could be the proximity of the devices, especially near the router, so move it, or switch to a speaker with less interference too.

Alexa isn't recognizing you

- Over time, you might start to notice that Alexa isn't acting as efficient as it used to. There are a few ways to fix this, and they are as follows.

- The first, is the obvious turning of the speaker off and on again. Sometimes a power cycle just fixes everything. If that doesn't work, try to move your speaker away from any obstacles and at least 8 inches away from your nearest wall.

- There is also the element of the seasons. Now, you might not realize this, but let's take for example you got your Echo in the winter. Maybe you don't use your heat all that much, and Alexa could hear you as clear as crystal.

  However, as time passes, and the summer hits, often we have the A/C blasting, and that could disrupt the ability of Alexa to hear you, especially if it's near the A/C. Simply put, if Alexa can't hear you, chances are it might just need to be away from the excess noises. This also applies not just to air conditioning, but also other appliances as well, such as a television, game system, or the like. Figure out the best place to put everything, and then make sure that it says consistent for the Alexa system.

- Finally, you can use the voice training part to try to fix this. What you do is go to the app, say 25 different phrases at your normal distance. This will help with Alexa further recognizing you.

Accidentally Activating It

- Now, this is kind of a humorous sort of situation, but it ties into the elements said before. You might have the moment where you have Alexa near a television, and suddenly, it starts to activate. You hear various devices turning on, and you start to wonder what it is that you can do about this. This can drive you plumb crazy, but there are a few solutions to this.

- The first, is to put Alexa away from speakers in general. This can be music, television, or even games. Just keep the system away from that. if you can, put it in a quiet room.

- Make sure as well that the voice recognition is there, because often, the reason why Alexa is picking up all this, is because it doesn't recognize you. make sure that you do the voice training in the app as needed.

- If anything, definitely a room change can make all the difference for you. Sometimes Alexa is able to pick up a lot of noise. It might also be the sensitivity of it, which can be fixed by checking the settlings and configuring it. it's a solution that can be fixed easily, or with a bit more depth to it, whatever you believe is fitting.

Your Echo Will Not Turn On

- Check to make sure that the Echo is plugged in properly. Make sure that the cord is plugged into the Echo properly, the cord should be fitted into the groove that can be found on the back of the device. It is also important to make sure that the device is plugged into the wall properly.
- Check the cord to make sure that it is not faulty. There should be no fraying, or areas that are damaged. If you do find that the cord is damaged, it should be replaced before the Echo is used.

Your Echo Will Not Connect to Your WiFi

- If your Echo will not connect to your WiFi, it could be that your Echo is too far away from the router. Keep the Echo away from walls, microwaves, baby monitors and cordless phones. Move your Echo closer to your router and see if it is able to connect.
- If your Echo still will not connect to your WiFi, you will want to first make sure that the password you are using is correct. Many times, just one letter is off, causing your Echo to not connect.
- You may find that you need to completely reboot your router if your Echo is not connecting. Simply turn the router off, unplug it from its

power source, count to 30 and then plug it back in. Allow time for all of the lights to come on before trying to connect your Echo.

Your Echo Will Not Connect to Bluetooth

- If your device is not within 30 feet of the Echo, the two will not be able to communicate with each other. Move the device closer and see if the Echo will connect.
- Check to see if the Bluetooth is enabled on your device. Check the Bluetooth settings on your device to ensure that Echo will be able to connect.
- The Echo may not be paired with your device. You have to pair Alexa with the device before you can connect with it. Choose the Echo on your Bluetooth menu in order to pair the two.

There is No Sound Coming from The Echo

- If the Echo is on and connected there are a few things that would cause it to be no sound. The first thing that you will want to do is check to ensure the Echo is not muted. Rotate the volume ring at the top of the Echo clockwise in order to turn the volume up.
- If you have been listening to your favorite music with the volume levels high, there is a good chance that you blew out the speakers. You may need to replace the speakers as well as the subwoofer and tweeter. If you have not had the volume turned up, you need to make sure that the device has not been dropped as this could break the speakers as well.

The Sound Coming from The Echo Is Distorted

- If the Echo does listen to commands and produce sound but the sound is distorted, there are a few things that could be causing the issue. One of these issues is that the tweeter is broken. If the sound coming from the Echo seems like there is too much bass, you might need to replace the tweeter.
- On the other hand, if you find that the sound coming from the Echo is too high pitched, it could be that the subwoofer is broken and needs to be replaced.

- If you find that the sound coming from the Echo is distorted in some other way, there are a few things that might need to be replaced including the speakers, power board and speaker driver board.

The Light Ring On The Echo Has Stopped Working

- If everything else on the Echo is working properly, but the light ring is not working, there is a high chance that the LED and Microphone board is not working and needs to be replaced.

The Echo Does Not Hear Your Commands

- If you have yelled at your Echo, pressed the action button and are still getting no reaction, the Echo may have turned its microphone off. If the microphone is off, the light ring will be red. In order to turn the microphone back on, simply press the microphone button on the top of the Echo.

It is not likely that you will face any issues with your Echo that you cannot solve on your own. As you probably noticed, most of the fixes to the problems that you might face are quite simple. However, if you do come across a problem that you cannot fix on your own or one that is not listed in this chapter, Amazon has great customer service and is more than happy to help you with your problem.

It is also important to remember that the Echo is a device, it is not a toy and it should not be played with. If you place your Echo in your home and do not move it around or drop it, chances are that you will not have any issues.

You cannot get your streaming services to stream

- One thing that people love about the Echo devices is that they are able to stream media from several different sources. If however, you are not able to stream, it is likely that you are dealing with some type of Wi-Fi interference. You may also not have fast enough internet or a firewall may be installed on your network.
- If you have an internet connection speed less than .5 MBPS, you are most likely not going to be able to stream anything effectively.

Chapter 12- How To Play Your Favorite Music and Watch Video On Echo

Did you know that you can stream any audio to the Echo? Well, it is true! From using the Echo as a speaker for your television to using it to stream your favorite music, the Echo is the perfect speaker!

One of the things that many people use the Echo for is to play their favorite music. Many people believe that their only option is to use the libraries that are available such as iHeart Radio or Amazon Music. Of course, the only music you can play from these libraries is music that you own.

However, what most people do not realize is that they can actually stream music from any device such as their cell phone and play it on the Echo.

Music Commands On Alexa

1. Alexa, play [artist] radio on Pandora or Spotify.
2. Alexa, Play Spotify
3. Alexa, Play Pop.
4. Alexa, pause.
5. “Alexa, Thumb up this song," or "Alexa, Thumb down this song.”
6. “Alexa, skip this song.”
7. Alexa, volume ten.

8. “Alexa, Pause/Stop/Play music.”
9. Alexa, stop the song.
10. “Alexa, volume up," or "Alexa, volume down.”
11. Alexa, resume.
12. "Alexa, what song is this?"
13. Alexa, play softer.
14. Alexa, next song.
15. Alexa, stop.

How to Pair Alexa To Any Devices with Bluetooth, So Echo Can Play Your Music

1. The first thing that you will want to do is to make sure that you have your Blue Tooth turned to the ON position on whatever device your music is located on.

2. The next step is to pair your device with Alexa. Most of us have paired with other devices before however if you haven't all you have to do is choose the Echo under the list of found devices. When you click on Echo, it will pair with your device.

3. All you have to do from there is start streaming your favorite music. The only catch is that when you are streaming music through a device, Alexa will not be able to pause, go back, go forward or stop the music, this must be done on the device.

Commands You Can Use Are:

"Alexa, Play"
"Alexa, Stop"
"Alexa, Pause"
"Alexa, Previous"
"Alexa, Next"
"Alexa, Resume"

Not only is this going to work with the music that is on your device but it is going to work with any audio. If you have a podcast that you want to listen to, play it through the Echo. If you have an audio book on your device, listen to it through the Echo.
Now, we can literally listen to anything that we want as long as we have it on one of our devices.

If for some reason you decide that you no longer want a device paired with your Echo, all that you have to do is open the Alexa app on your cell phone or go to the Echo website, choose settings and then select the device that you want to remove at the top of the page. From this point, you will choose Bluetooth and then click clear. The device will be removed and no longer paired with your Echo.

This comes in handy if you want to sell your device or if you are upgrading to a new one. Another benefit of being able to stream audio from your devices is that if you are having people over to your house, they can pair their devices with your Echo and play music off of their devices. When the part is over, all you have to do is unpair the devices. This means that you don't have to worry about ensuring you have music that everyone will like, let them bring some of their own.

On top of this, you can use your smart TV and the Echo to stream the audio from Netflix, Hulu, and other channels which will make it easier for you hear the audio from every room in your house.

It is important, while you are streaming any type of audio but especially music that you do not turn the volume up too high. If you are playing music with a lot of bass, it could blow out your speakers very easily. Even if the music does not have a lot of bass, playing it too loudly could damage the speakers.

If you think that there has been damage done to the speakers, the first thing that you need to do is make sure that the Echo has not been muted. If the Echo has not been muted, please see the troubleshooting section of this book for more information.

Now, if you do have Amazon Music. You can get music from there, and you can also link it to your

Pandora and Spotify accounts if you've got premium.

Connect Your Echo with Other Music Services

Set up Pandora for Alexa

Here are the simple steps to get your started using Pandora quickly:

1. Open your Alexa app, then tap on Music, Video & Book, choose Pandora, then from the Pandora registration page, tap "Link your account Now"
2. If you have Pandora account, simple just enter your account email and password to link it.
3. If you are new to Pandora, you need to complete the registration form. That's it. Now Alexa can play your stations.

Set Up Spotify For Alexa

How to do this is simple, and the steps are as follows:

- Open Alexa App
- Go to "Music, Video and Books"

- Select Spotify,
- Link the accounts
- Say "Alexa, play Spotify

Change Your Music Preferences

1. Open your Alexa app,
2. Go to **setting**, then **Music & Media**.
3. Tap **Choose Default Music Services**, choose the service you like, then select **Done.**

Link iHeartRadio to Echo

1. Open your Alexa App.
2. Go to **Settings,** then **Music & Media**.
3. Select iHeartRadio and link it to your Amazon Echo.

The Echo Show as well as the Echo Spot allows you to watch videos on the touchscreens.

You can watch all sorts of videos on the Echo Show though. For example, you can watch movie trailers, cooking shows, and so much more.

The great news is that you don't have to do anything special in order to watch your videos. Just tell Alexa what you are looking for. There are skills however, that you can use if you want to connect your smart television to the Echo devices. When you do this, you can tell Alexa what you want to watch on which television and it will play for you as long as you have a television service that is currently playing that specific show. This works great with Amazon TV.

Chapter 13- How To Use Alexa For Your Business

Have you ever taken the time to think about all that we have to accomplish each day? Of course, if you think about all that we expect of ourselves, it is no wonder that all of it is not getting done. However, it can all get done with the help of our personal assistant Alexa.

Alexa is a huge help for those of us who have a tone to do and not enough hours in our day to get them all done. Alexa has many different productivity skills that are going to help you save time, work smarter, and face the tasks that must be done each day. Alexa is able to change your life for the better.

Alexa has many different productivity skills that are going to help you get your day to day tasks completed quickly and on time. While there are many different productivity skills, I want to go over just a few of the best with you.

Alexa is also going to allow you to send a text message via your voice. All you have to do as you are making your coffee in the morning is to tell Alexa to send the message for you.

Most of us know that conference calls are not always as productive as they could be however, Alexa can take some of the time out of the call. Alexa is able to dial in your conference call information, input your ID and then once you are connected, Alexa can call you. All you have to do is to answer and suddenly you are taking part in the call.

You can also leave a voicemail using Bulletin Board. When a person is checking their Bulletin Board, they will be able to hear the message.

The Echo can help you run your business better. One of the things that many people who are using the Echo in their office love is that they no longer have to worry about **running out of office supplies.**

It does not matter if you have a home office or an office away from home, we all need office supplies. The great thing about having the Echo in your office is that you can add the supplies to your shopping list as you notice that they are getting low, have Alexa order them and before you know it Amazon will be shipping them to your home or office.

The Echo is able to use popular office software such as Google Calendar to ensure that you know exactly what needs to be done when. Not only is Google Calendar a great app for using at home but it is great for using with your business as well.

For example, if you have a home business, you can schedule tasks that need to be completed each day as well as tasks that you need to complete at home. You can schedule meetings, classes, and even doctor's appointments. As we discussed earlier in this book, all you have to do is to have Alexa add an event to your calendar but make sure you check it regularly to ensure you are not scheduling more than one task at a time.

The Echo is also able to sort through your email for you as well as read it and respond. No matter what type of business you are in, chances are that you have emails that need to be answered and they need to be answered in a timely manner. The Echo is able to sort through the email, searching for important emails from your clients, while you spend your time focusing on other important tasks. The Echo can then read the email to you and respond for you.

On top of this, the Echo is going to be able to watch Facebook and Twitter for posts that mention certain words, such as the name of your business or the product that you offer. **When the Echo finds these posts, it can alert you to them ensuring that you know what is being posted about your product**. You will also be able to respond to these posts or tweets.

Echo is also able to transcribe conversations for you. Instead of recording a conversation and having someone transcribe it later, all you have to do is tell the Echo to transcribe the conversation while it is taking place. The Echo will transcribe the conversation and send it to you in a Word document.

Just like people use Echo to create a smart home, you can use Echo to create a smart office as well. You can program the Echo so that when you leave the office at night, the computers go to sleep and all of the lights to go out. In the same manner, you can program it so that all of the lights come on and the computers wake up when you come in each morning.

How else can the Echo help you with your business? We all know that many people are working from home today and it seems to be the way of the future.
The problem with this is, many people do not have the self-discipline that it takes to work from home. It is so easy to get distracted or to even forget a certain client's requirements. Let's start with distractions.

Alexa is able to help you stay on task because you can use it as a timer. Anyone who has worked at home or for themselves knows that it is important to set timers if you want to be productive**. For example, many people will work one hour and then take 10 minutes off and repeat this cycle until all of their work is completed. It helps them to stay focused**. You can use Alexa as that timer, ensuring that you do not lose track of time, that you are working the full hour and that you are only taking 10 minutes off at a time.

Moving on to a client's requirements, all you have to do is have Alexa take a note of what each of your clients requests. When you have an order from that specific client, simply ask Alexa what their requirements are. That way, you won't find yourself with upset clients because you forgot to complete the task the way they requested.

You can also create daily to-do lists, have Alexa mark items off of the to-do list, have Alexa tell you what is next on your to-do list and if you are a more visual person like I am, you can have Alexa send you the list via your email.

List of Alexa skills that can help you

If you are having a hard time feeling motivated, let Alexa know and it will provide you with <u>motivational quotes</u> as well as a few suggestions that might help you get started.

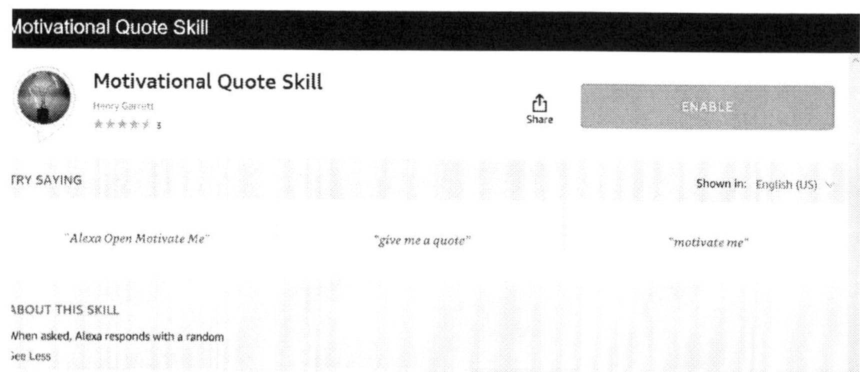

Most people have heard of Dragon Speak Easy by now, which is a program that types as you speak, saving you all of the hard work of typing up whatever it is that you are creating. However, what a lot of people do not know is that they can use the Echo to create documents as well, simply by speaking out what they want to be typed.

This means that if you need to create a letter but don't feel like typing it up, simply tell Alexa that you want to dictate a letter. Once the letter has been completed it will be sent to you in a word document for you to proofread, print out and send.

There are so many different ways that Alexa can help, from letting you know when you have an order, to keeping track of all of the products that you have in stock, and even let you know how much you are earning. Alexa truly is the secretary that you never had and never thought that you would be able to find.

Of course, there are many different skills that you can use to help you with your business, job and even dealing with those bad days.

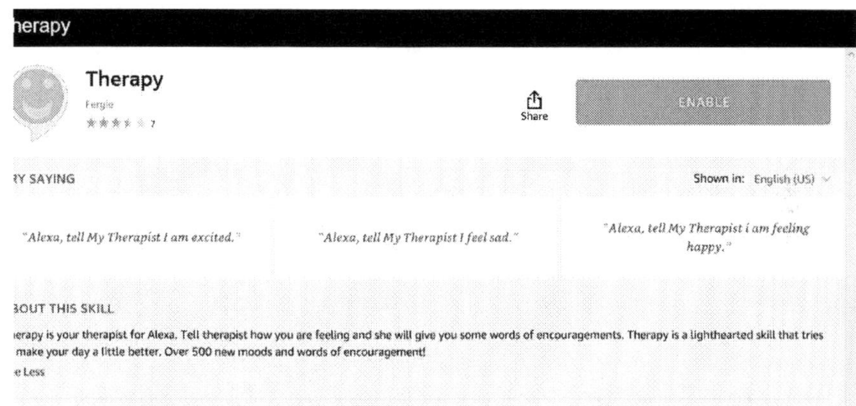

One skill that many people who are running their own businesses enjoy using is the <u>Therapy skill.</u>
When you use this skill, you will be able to vent to Alexa about your day while getting a bit of helpful advice as well. So instead of going home or walking out of your office filled with pent up emotions, use Alexa to get them out.
There is even a skill that will give you all the business advice that you need without you ever having to hire a personal coach.

Simply head over to the skills website and click on the business/finance tab to find all of the different skills that are available to you.

Chapter 14- How To Make Echo Your Smart Home Hub

Smart Home Device Set Up

People love the Echo because it provides you with a personal assistant that does what you ask as soon as you ask. However, what people love the most about the Echo is that they are able to link multiple devices to the Echo and control them with the sound of your voice.

By doing this, you are able to create a smart home that does exactly what you want when you want it to. For example, if you want to watch a specific on television, all you have to do is to tell Alexa to play it. Perhaps you want to make sure the doors are locked but don't want to get out of bed. All you have to do is to tell Alexa to do it for you.

You can fill your home with many different smart devices which you can then control using your Alexa app or your voice but what is really amazing is that you can have your devices communicate with each other.

In order to do this, you are going to need to use the service IFTTT (if this then that). This service is going to provide you with what is called premade recipes which will allow you to connect your devices to each other. You can then use IFTTT to program your devices, create routines, have your devices react to triggers, or send commands to your other devices.

One example of this would be to turn off your lights. Perhaps it is too cold for you go outside and switch off your Christmas lights. If you have connected your lights to the Belkin WeMo switch then you can use the IFTTT recipe to control them with your voice.

Or maybe you have laid your phone down somewhere in your home and don't know where it is. All you have to do is to ask Alexa to make it ring for you.

There are even smart LED lights which change color. You can use the IFTTT recipe to put them on a loop to make them change color during a party.

IFTTT can even help you with workouts. You can use the seven-minute workout skill in order to ensure you are getting the most out of your workouts!

But let's take a step back. Almost everything in your home, your lights, garage doors, thermostat, washer, and air conditioner can be controlled by using your Echo device or your Alexa app.

There are so many different accessories which only work with certain products. Some of them work better than others and it can be a little confusing.

When you are purchasing your smart home products you need to make sure that they say "Works with Alexa" on them. The Echo is the best way for you to turn your home into a smart home because the Echo works with more of the smart home items than the other virtual assistants do.

In order to set up the smart home accessories you will have to have the Alexa app downloaded to your phone. The Alexa app is going to allow you to add the skills that you will need in order to ensure that you are able to use the smart home accessories.

Connect Smart Device With Alexa

1. Open Alexa App, Go to "smart Home"

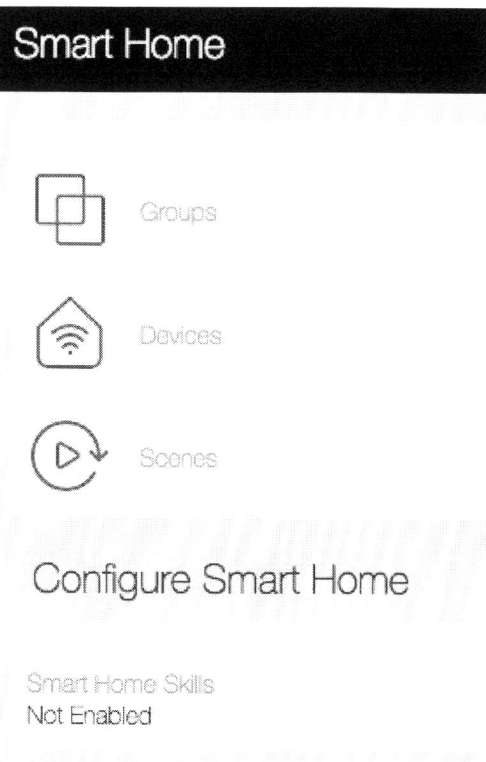

2. Now Enable the skill for the device you want to use with Echo by tapping on “Smart Home Skill”

3. Now you need to pair the device with Echo, just tell Alexa **"Alexa, discover Device"**, and wait for the process to be completed. OR do it from app by selecting "**Device**" and choose "**discover**"

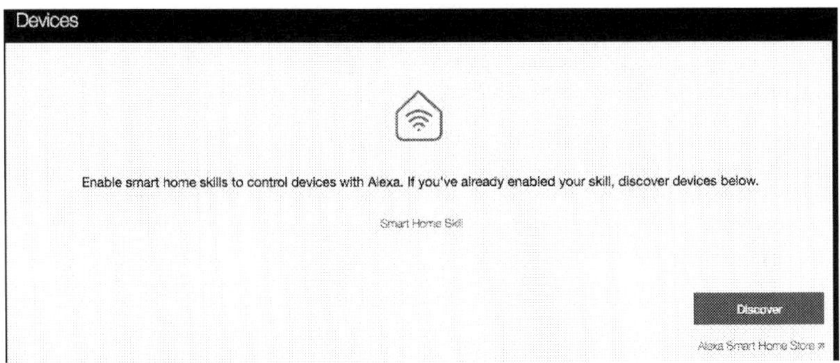

Smart Home Device That Compatible With Alexa

Lock Front Door

August Smart Lock: you can buy this lock, enable the skill and connect it with Alexa, now you can ask Alexa to lock the front door for you.

Turn The Lights On and Off with Alexa

Philips hue system: Turning the lights on and off is pretty simple, and the steps to do so are listed as follows:

- Open up the Alexa app
- Update the software for any smart home devices if necessary before you add them to Alexa

- Go to the smart home section of the Alexa app
- Make sure that all of your names are tweaked in the system. For example, if you have two front porch lights, it's important that you name them "front porch one" and "front porch two" respectively
- Once at the smart home tab, you'll have these choices. **Groups, Smart home skills, Devices and Scenes.** The smart home products require you to enable the skill for them to work, then you must search the device with the echo. To start, go to **Devices**, and then discover devices.
- If it's a **Philips hue system**, you'll need to tap the button on the bridge of the hue to connect it, but for others, there might not be a physical step.
- Simply talk to Alexa and she'll turn the lights on and off for you.

"Alexa, turn on my living room."

"Alexa, turn off the kitchen light"

"Alexa, dim the office."

Now, these voice commands are a bit different, especially with some of the name brands, so it's important that you know a bit about how the Alexa system works before you try this. However, you can tell Alexa to turn the bedroom lights on, or turn the bathroom lights to 50%, which is half the lights. You can do this with really any percentage, and it's similar to those lights in rooms where you control with a dial, except without the dial anymore.

Smart Plug

One very useful product that has been created to work with the Echo is the **Smart Plug.** The Smart Plug sells for about 25 dollars and connects wirelessly to your Echo. It can be used to turn electronics that plug into a regular wall plug on an off. Examples would be a light or a fan.

Once you plug the Smart Plug into the wall, you will want to download the skill called, *Kasa*, which will detect your Smart Plug and connect it to your WiFi.

Then you can connect the Smart Plug to your Echo and give the device a name, such as "end table lamp 1." When you tell Alexa to turn on end table lamp 1, and the lamp will turn on.

There are even smart home kits that can do many different types of things such as detect a water leak or motion. These sell for about 250 dollars each.

Lamps and fans are not the only things that you can control with your Echo. If you purchase smart light bulbs, the Echo will recognize them just as it would the Smart Plug. You will be able to name the lights, for example, "Kitchen lights." When you want the lights turned on or off, all you have to do is to tell Alexa to do so.

Using Thermostat With Alexa

Nest controller thermostat: To tell Alexa to turn on the thermostat, you simply do the following:

- Install smart home thermostat.
- Go to the Alexa app

- Either search for the smart home devices by discovering the device or You can wait for Alexa to search for this
- Synch up the thermostat to the system, making sure that it has the fitting name.
- You can then go to the "Groups" tab in the Smart Home system, giving you a chance to program and set the devices to the various groups you want them to be. This is especially important if you have various rooms with one controlled by Echo.
- If you're using a **Nest controller thermostat**, there is the thermostat controller skill, which you can search for. This will give you a chance to have more functionality with a Nest appliance. With this, you can directly ask Alexa what the temperature is, allowing you to set it.

Control Your Television

Logitech's Harmony Hub: Just following the setting up step mentioned above, now you can use Alexa to turn on/off your TV and gaming system that connected to the hub, launch specific channel.

Control Your Speaker With Alexa

Sonos Speaker: for now, you need to physical connect it to your Echo using a stereo cable, with the speaker on, you can hear Alexa more clearly, and play your music at a much higher volume.

Voice Commands To Control Your Smart Home

"Alexa, turn on the lights"
"Alexa, turn off the kitchen lights"
"Alexa, dim the lights"
Alexa, set the temperature to 72"
"Alexa, lock my front door."
"Alexa, discover my device"
"Alexa, raise the temperature 1 degree"
"Alexa, turn on/off the TV"

If you have GE appliances with the Geneva skill:

"Alexa, ask Geneva if my laundry is dry"
"Alexa, tell Geneva to preheat my oven to [your preferred degree].

What about other electronics, more advanced devices such as your dishwasher?

The Echo can now control a few GE appliances. Many of us dream of being able to tell our appliances what to do without ever having to get up but now, **that dream is becoming a reality.**

This new technology is going to work with about 70 different GE models, including washing machines, dryers, dishwashers, refrigerators, ranges, and ovens. These models were already able to connect to WiFi before the Echo was released, which made it easy for GE to create a skill enabling you to control them with just your voice.

Imagine being able to preheat your oven with just the sound of your voice or being able to find out how much time until the load of laundry is finished drying without ever having to leave your seat!

While older models of the appliances cannot connect to the Echo, the newer models that are WiFi enabled will have no problem connecting. Not only are you going to be able to control your appliances while not having to get up from your chair but imagine if you were cooking dinner and had your hands stuck in a bowl mixing it when you realized you needed to preheat the oven. It would be much easier to just use voice commands than it would to clean your hands, set the preheat and then get back to mixing.

Of course, there are going to be some things that GE will not let the Echo have control over, for example, turning on the stove top burners. The reason for this is simply because it would not be safe.

The good news when it comes to controlling your appliances with the Echo is that there is nothing new to buy. All you have to do is download the skill and your appliances are already ready to go.

One of the newer advances that the Echo has made is the ability to connect with your smart TV. Now, all you have to do is tell Alexa to find the show that you want to watch, and without you ever having to pick up the remote controller, your television will switch right to that show.

In reality, we are a long way from having fully voice controlled homes. While we do have robots that sweep our floors, televisions that connect to the internet and now appliances that turn on by voice command, there is still a long way to go.

What people are finding, however, is that the Echo is leading the way when it comes to developing these smart homes and what they love the most about it is that they are able to turn their current home into the smart home of their dreams.

Chapter 15- Update, Reset, Change Setting and Helpful Tips

let's move on to some tips and tricks that are going to help you when it comes to using your Echo.

Update Echo

The Echo is supposed to update every night, however if you are looking for a specific update, for example, some of the older Echo's did not come with the ability to control appliances, you will want to force and update. In order to do this, press the mute button on the Echo and hold it down for 30 seconds. When you release the mute button, the Echo will begin to update.

Creating Group

You don't have to name every single light in your home or every single lamp. For example, if you have three ceiling lights in your living room, you can create a group on the Alexa app, naming all three lights, "Living room lights." When you tell Alexa to turn them on, off, dim or brighten them, the Echo will control all of the lights at the same time.

Add accounts to family profile

If there your entire household does not share the same Amazon account. There are multiple accounts for multiple people, you can add these accounts to your family profile. When different members of the family want to use the Echo, all they have to do is tell Alexa to switch the accounts. However, you need to be careful when doing this. The Echo will not create separate calendars or to-do lists for the different profiles and all of the profiles will be able to order from the Amazon Prime account.

Change Wake-up word

Some people may not like the wake-up word, “Alexa” and may decide that they want to choose a different wake-up word. You can instead, choose to use “Echo” as the wake-up word if you go to echo.amazon.com and click on settings. You will choose your Echo, click on the wake word tab and choose which option you want to use.

Changing the voice setting

Everything that you say to Alexa is going to be recorded as well as uploaded to the Amazon servers, however, if you are not comfortable with the idea of there being hundreds of recordings of your voice floating around out there, you do have the option of deleting them. Simply go to amazon.com/myx. Sign in and then click on your Echo. Once this is done, you will click on the manage voice settings tab.

How to correctly giving Alexa commands

When you are giving Alexa commands, you do not need to pause after stating your wake-up word. For example, you do not need to say, "Alexa," and then wait for the light on the Echo to come on. You can say the entire command without pausing and the Echo will do as it is told.

How to turn off the microphone

Let's imagine that you are having company over and one of the guest's name is Alexa... Chances are that you do not want your Echo listening for the name Alexa and listening for commands every time someone says the name. If this happens, all you have to do is turn off the microphone by pressing and holding the microphone button until the LED light on the Echo turns red. When you are ready to turn the microphone back on, simply press the microphone button again.

Recently releases skills

If you are interested in the most recently releases skills, you can search for them on the skills page by changing the way that they are sorted, according to the release date. Or, you can simply ask Alexa what the most recent released skills are.

Reset Your Echo to Factory Default

If you Echo is unresponsive, you can reset it to factory default by following these steps:

1. Make sure you press and hold the Microphone off and Volume down buttons together, wait about (20 seconds), the light ring will turn orange. After that it will turn blue.
2. You need to wait for the light ring to turn itself off and on again, and then it turns back to orange, at this step, you Echo enters the setup mode.
3. Now, open your Alexa app and start the setup steps: Connect Echo to your WIFI and register it to Amazon account.

Helpful Tips

1. Many people do not realize just how much Amazon loves to reward their customers and that means that when you become the owner of an Echo, Amazon is going to reward you. Amazon does this by sending you exclusive deals that are not available to the general public.

2. It is very important for you to always tell on Alexa when it does not do what you tell it to. There are going to be times when the Echo does not understand what you are saying or it gets your command completely wrong. Amazon wants to know when Alexa is not behaving properly so that they can fix it and ensure that their customers are happy with the service they are receiving.

3. If you are running late for work and missed your bus, you can tell Alexa to book you a ride with Uber. If you have a ride already booked and are wondering when your ride is going to arrive at your house, all you have to do is ask Alexa where your ride is and it will provide you with an expected time of arrival.

The Echo seems to be changing and evolving every single day. However, all of these tips and tricks are going to ensure that you are up to date on the latest updates and that you are getting the most out of your Echo. After all, we all want to get the most out of the items that we have paid for.

If you really want to get the most use out of your Amazon Echo, I suggest that you spend some time playing around with it, experimenting with different skills and trying to incorporate it into every area of your life.

Let every member of your family enjoy the Echo, let it answer all of the questions that you never had answers to, **let it be your therapist, your assistant, your sous chef and more.**

When you find that you are having a hard time in any area of your life, chances are that the Echo has a skill that is going to be able to help you, to make your life easier and to reduce the amount of stress that you are dealing with. **What more could we ask for from such a little device?**

Chapter 16 - The Best 250 Easter Eggs You Can Ask Alexa

This chapter is simply a list of the Easter Eggs that people have found for the Amazon Echo. What is an Easter Egg? These are commands that you can use, which most people don't know about, but that will give you a response from Alexa that you will enjoy.

Remember as you give each of these commands, you must begin with Alexa. Only then, with the Echo wake up and listen to what you are saying.

Asking Personal Questions with Alexa

1. Are you a robot?
2. Are you my mummy?
3. Are you tired
4. Say you're sorry.
5. Are you in love?
6. You complete me
7. Do you have any relatives?
8. Give me a kiss
9. Who loves ya, baby?

10. Who is the boss
11. Never gonna give you up.
12. Do you know Siri
13. Where do you want to be when you grow up?
14. Take me to your leader
15. Do you want to kiss?
16. Do you have a last name?
17. What is your dream job?
18. Who is your role model?
19. What is your favorite city?
20. What make you happy?
21. What is your favorite ice cream?
22. Are you human?
23. Do you have a job
24. What are you thankful for?
25. What is your favorite food?
26. Who is your daddy?
27. What can you do?
28. Why so serious?
29. Do you believe in love at first sight?
30. Do you have any brothers and sisters?
31. How tall are you?
32. Where do you live?
33. Who is your best friend?

34. Do you love me?
35. Are you smart?
36. Do you have a partner?
37. Were you sleeping?
38. How old are you?

Asking Funny Questions

1. Can you give me some money?
2. Who let the dogs out?
3. Knock Knock.
4. Party on Wayne.
5. Roll the dice.
6. Pick a random number between x and y.
7. Tell me a joke.
8. Are you lying?
9. What is the sound of one hand clapping?
10. See ya later alligator.
11. Do you like your name?
12. Are you an eavesdropping device?
13. Am I pretty?
14. Do you smoke?
15. Are you thirsty?

16. Can you see me?
17. What are you made of?
18. Why were you made?
19. I'm tired.
20. I'm hungry.
21. I'm sad.
22. You're silly.
23. Sing me a song.
24. You hurt me.
25. Ask me something.
26. Where do babies come from?
27. Say the alphabet
28. Do you have a boyfriend?
29. Do you want to fight?
30. Do you want to build a snowman?
31. I think you're funny
32. May the force be with you?
33. I'm home
34. Can I ask a question?
35. Tell me something interesting
36. How high can you count?
37. You're wonderful
38. Are you happy?
39. One fish, two fish

40. What number are you thinking of?
41. What is best in life?
42. Good night
43. Say a bad word
44. Happy holidays
45. Sorry
46. Can you smell that?
47. Will pigs fly?
48. Do you dream?
49. Tesing 1-2-3
50. Are you connected to the internet?
51. Are you crazy?
52. Are you female?
53. Who is the fairest of them all?
54. Are you real?
55. Are you okay?
56. Are you stupid?
57. Can you lie?
58. Can you smell that?
59. Cheers!
60. Did you get my email?
61. Do you have a last name?
62. Do you want to go on a date?

63. Guess what?
64. Ha ha!
65. Happy Christmas
66. Happy New Year
67. Honey, I'm home
68. How do you boil an egg?
69. How much does the earth weight?
70. I want the truth
71. Is there life on other planets?
72. Mac or PC?
73. Make me some coffee
74. One fish, two fish
75. Play it again, Sam
76. Roses are red.Say, Cheese!
77. Thank you
78. Up Up, Down Down, Left Right, Left Right, B, A, Start
79. What are you going to do today?
80. What do you want to be when you grow up?
81. What is love?
82. Why is the sky blue?
83. Will you marry me tomorrow?
84. You are so intelligent
85. You're wonderful

Top 15 Amazon Alexa Easter Eggs

1. What is the meaning of life?
2. Is there a Santa?
3. What is the best tablet?
4. Make me a sandwich.
5. What is your favorite color?
6. I am your father.
7. What is the loneliest number?
8. How much is the doggie in the window?
9. Beam me up.
10. Who's your daddy?
11. What is your quest?
12. Who is the fairest of them all?
13. To be or not to be?
14. Who ya gonna call?
15. Do you have any brothers or sisters?

Miscellaneous Easter Eggs

1. Random fact
2. What's your birthday?
3. What's the answer to life, the universe, and everything?

4. Who stole the cookies from the cookie jar?
5. Will pigs fly?
6. What is your IQ?
7. What color are your eyes?
8. Do you speak any other languages?
9. What are you wearing
10. There is no moon?
11. How much does the earth weigh?
12. Surely you can't be serious
13. Night Night.
14. What do you think about Cortana?
15. How much wood can a woodchuck chuck if a woodchuck could chuck wood?
16. Where have all the flowers gone?
17. I want the truth
18. Make me breakfast
19. Is the cake a lie?
20. What is a day without sunshine?
21. Why do birds suddenly appear?
22. Hello it's me
23. Do you like green eggs and ham
24. Winter is coming
25. It's a trap
26. Who loves orange soda

27. Who lives in a pineapple under the sea
28. Where am I?
29. High five.
30. Are you alive?
31. It's a bird! It's a plane!
32. Cook me dinner
33. What does a cat say?
34. I have a cold
35. Why are there so many songs about rainbows?
36. Will it snow tomorrow?
37. Did you miss me?
38. Where are my glasses?
39. What is my mission
40. Divide by zero
41. Do you know everything?
42. Who is your inspiration
43. When is the first day of spring
44. Is this the real life?
45. Do the dishes
46. Why do you sit there like that
47. Twinkle, twinkle, little star
48. What time is sunrise?
49. Can we be friends?

50. Thumbs down
51. Don't listen to him!
52. How many teeth do sharks have?
53. Can reindeer fly?
54. Who is the shortest person in the world?
55. Do .... Or do not
56. Can you tell me how to get to the sesame street?
57. I don't know
58. What does the dog say?
59. Where's the beef?
60. Entertain me
61. How do I connect Bluetooth?
62. Life is like a box of chocolates
63. How old am I?
64. How old is my sister?
65. What is X plus Y?
66. Heads or Tails?
67. What is a noun?
68. Where is Italy
69. What is the prime number?
70. Live long and prosper
71. Show me the money
72. Tea. Earl Grey. Hot
73. Why is six afraid of seven?

74. What is the sound of one hand clapping?
75. Can you touch me?
76. What are the 5 greatest words in the English language?
77. Can I tell you a secret?
78. Who is your best friend?
79. What is happiness?
80. What size shoe do you wear?
81. Are you working?
82. Sing happy birthday
83. Am I funny?
84. Tell me a poem
85. Do a barrel roll.
86. Show me the TV.
87. Count by ten
88. Simon say [anything]. (echo will repeat what you say, try this)
89. Say hello to my little friend!
90. What is the loneliest number?
91. How many roads must a man walk down?
92. Remeo, remeo, wherefore art thou remeo?
93. Who won the best actor Oscar in 1973?
94. How many licks does it take to get to the center of a tootsie pop?

95. Where's waldo?
96. Is the tooth fairy real?
97. Where are my keys? (ask twice)
98. Ya feel me?
99. What's your birthday?
100. Have you ever seen the rain?
101. Who is Eliza?
102. Speak!
103. We all scream for ice cream!
104. I'll be back
105. Happy thanksgiving
106. What are the seven wonders of the world?
107. This statement is false
108. Who is on 1st?
109. Tell me a tongue twister
110. Which came first, the chicken or the egg?
111. Who's going to win the Super Bowl?

Funny Music Questions

4. Alexa, Daisy Daisy.
5. Alexa, do you know the muffin man?
6. Alexa, do you really want to hurt me?
7. Alexa, Hello, It's Me.
8. Alexa, I like big butts."
9. Alexa, is this the real life?
10. Alexa, never gonna give you up
11. Alexa, sing me a song.
12. Alexa, sing me a song.
13. Alexa, twinkle, twinkle little star.
14. Alexa, what is love?
15. Alexa, what is war good for?
16. Alexa, where have all the flowers gone?
17. Alexa, who let the dogs out?
18. Alexa, who stole the cookies from the cookie jar?
19. Alexa, why do birds suddenly appear?

There are many more and who knows, ask Alexa some questions of your own, maybe you will find a few. Of course, more Easter Eggs are being found every single day and posted on Echo forums. You never really know what answer you will get from Alexa.

Conclusion

It is amazing how much Alexa and the Echo devices can do. What is wonderful about the Echo devices is that because they all use Alexa, they are all set up basically the same way and they are all controlled the same way. This means that you don't have to have a new book telling you how to get the most out of each and every Echo device.

I hope that this book has helped you learn how to use your Echo device and get the most out of it every single day. I hope that you have learned how you can use Alexa to make your life easier and I hope that somehow this book has made it easier for you to understand Alexa.

Alexa and the Echo devices can make your life easier and it can make your life run smoother however, this is only going to happen if you know how to take advantage of all of Alexa and the Echo devices benefits. By using the information that you have learned in this book, you are going to be able make sure that you know how to use all of the features and that you know how to have a little bit of fun with Alexa.

Alexa: 2018 Amazon Alexa User Guide

The Complete User Guide With Step-By-Step Instructions. Make The Most Of Alexa Today

36208657R00103

Made in the USA
Lexington, KY
12 April 2019